When 1 + 1 = 1

That "Impossible" Connection

Gabriela "la Moldava" Condrea

Paint with Words Press

2011

Published by Paint with Words Press

Book layout, cover art and design created and copyrighted © 2011 by Gabriela Condrea. Author photo with Morena Chiodi taken by Celeste Voria.

ISBN-13: 978-0-983-90630-8
ISBN-10: 0-983-90630-0

Printed in the United States of America

Contents

Introduction: Why connection?[1]

Connection. This theme of connection is something that has been with me all my life. I was six years old when we left the then Soviet Republic of Moldova for a distant place, to build a new life. I still remember the image of my cousin Mărioara chasing the train on the platform as we pulled away. On our way out of Chişinău, we passed by the hill behind the apartment where I spent the first six years of my life, and that is the first image I remember bringing me to tears when I returned to visit for the first time 14 years later. I remember wishing that my family was closer – yearning for a big family gathering. Immigration spread my mother's family across Europe and my father's family to Israel and Australia. We ended up in Seattle, on yet another continent. Large family gatherings are few and far between.

There have also been some relationships and non-relationships, connections and disconnections, romantically – the tug between career and love and the wanderings of a traveling soul. I've begun adopting cousins and brothers, sisters and aunts in distant places – connecting with people across oceans and time zones. Despite the geographic complications and even if we don't talk often, when we do finally get together or exchange a few messages, it's as if we saw each other yesterday. This stretching of ties to people is perhaps a reflection of the diaspora within me.

Tango has helped me connect with and understand myself in ways that in this society of staunch individualism, I had found hard to do. Of course in tango there are egos and hard-held opinions and divisions – all the traits you

[1] Inspired by a question from Paul Stieger of Boise, Idaho, USA in October 2012: "I'm most curious to ask, has the connection theme of your book been something growing inside you your whole life? Did the connection drive kick into an even higher gear when you began Tango in 2009?"

will find in most groups where people are passionate about what they do – but there is also an amazing feeling of community, of coexistence that is so palpable, of cooperation and interaction and respect between people that span generations. Through tango I've found a sense of belonging that I have struggled with, that many of us struggle with.

And, although tango is very special to me, it's not unique. It's not unique in the fact that it gives people an excuse to gather. Many activities do that and many more used to be prevalent in our society. Nowadays, when we sit in boxes at a desk, each staring at our own shiny little box, counting the minutes until we each climb into wheeled boxes all facing in one direction to reach our bigger boxes and lock the door behind us, how often do we really stop to touch, take a minute to listen to another person's heart, pause enough to acknowledge another person's story? When our stimuli are overwhelmingly visual and verbal and truth is concrete and quantified, how often do we recognize our troubles reflected in another's anguish? How often do we feel and trust our intuition?

We are empathetic by nature. I've been hearing of more and more studies that confirm this. For hundreds of years, we have been separated and divided. Man is self-serving and self-interested. His selfishness will lead your neighbor to steal from you, Hobbes told us. Survival of the fittest. But his empathy for another human being will also prompt your neighbor to get his saw when a tree falls on your house (as my friend Karl told me recently), empathy will tug at his heart when he sees an animal mistreated, and empathy is what will bring someone who has just enough money to buy food through the end of the week to still find a quarter to share with someone in need.

It's especially in the difficult times, in the vulnerable times that we can see the strength of our bonds with those around us – the connection – more clearly. When we lose a loved one, when we take a risk, when we dive into a dream without knowing where we're going – those are the moments when people stretch out a hand for us to hold, offer a warm welcome, join together to give us a push along our path. It's when we have the opportunity to help someone that we connect more deeply with our own humanity.

Tango has been an adventure as much outward as it has been inward. A journey to find myself, an excavation of the nerves and the emotions I had begun to trim and cut away – to numb myself to heartache, to shield myself from vulnerability, to protect myself from the unknown. Tango has seen me through some stunningly beautiful moments and some deeply painful moments – through loss and growth and adversity – through emotions that span the breadth of the gamut: from elation, uncontrolled, overwhelming joy to the sad, silent emptiness that's left when nothing else is. Tango has helped me see myself from the inside, out.

Can we separate the journey from the catalyst, from the propellers, from the person? I don't think so. It's all connected. It's all one package. We are all much more than black and white – we are many, many shades of gray. Tango has helped me understand that Life is About the Connection – with those around us and consequently, with ourselves.

A love affair with tango

Like most love affairs, it happened when I least expected it. I took a year off from teaching 8th grade in Seattle and went to volunteer in Perú, thinking that somehow I might find my way to Santiago de Chile and then maybe to Buenos Aires, to get a job in a restaurant and hang out for a while, maybe even learn to dance some salsa or something. To me, tango was that hold a rose in your teeth and walk in a sharp line back and forth image I had seen on TV. I really had no idea and little interest in finding out.

We met on February 22nd, 2009. It was a Sunday night, my first in Buenos Aires, at Armenia 1366. With our first embrace, I knew that this was different.

And we danced and danced and danced: in the subway, on the bus, in a plaza with a clown, on a small stage at a restaurant in La Boca, at concerts, at *milongas*.[2] Along the way I found people to share an embrace with, people to share my love of this dance with, and people to philosophize about life with. And even though I had to rest my feet when they went on strike, I knew that I was where I needed to be as we glided across the wooden floor of the small, square room of the studio.[3]

I feel so fortunate to have met tango. So fortunate to have found a passion, a reason to make sacrifices, a release, an asylum, a good friend, a philosophy, a language for communicating without words, a means of getting closer to myself.

I do, tango, for better or for worse, I do.

---

[2] *milonga* – a social gathering where people dance tango and other dances, such as the dance that's also called *milonga*

[3] When I say "the studio" I'm referring to the Dinzel Studio in Buenos Aires where I grew up as a tango dancer, my home away from home, created and owned by Gloria and Rodolfo Dinzel.

Tango is About the Connection

el abrazo[4]

I press my hand
against the line
of his back
pulling him closer
yet pushing him away
keeping him at a distance
creating the tension
the connection
defining the parameters
between two
who walk as one.

---

[4] *el abrazo* – an embrace, a hug

When 1+1=1

when the limits of our bodies
become obsolete and insignificant,
when each pulse of his chest
manifests itself through my legs,
when I can't tell if the sweat is his or mine,
and we move together as one...

Mejor que sola – Better than alone

I met up with Angel one night to share a bottle of wine and the harmonies of guitars and baritone voices. He knew I had come here for tango; that's why he had chosen this tiny bar where heaps of people gathered just to listen and sing along.

Afterward, he offered to accompany me on my walk home. *"Mejor que sola,"* I told him – better than walking alone.[5] He laughed, offended. It became an on-going joke between us. Of course he took it as: sure, you just don't want to walk by yourself at night on the streets of Buenos Aires. And he was partially right. But in general, I'd rather walk by myself than be in bad company. I enjoy my own company. I value my me-time.

If I say that sharing time with someone is better than being alone, in my mind, that's saying a lot.

---

[5] When I put text in **Spanish** first, it's because I originally wrote it in Spanish or because I like it in Spanish. In some cases, I offer an artistic rather than a direct translation, to better express the ideas that might otherwise be lost in translation.

More than the sum of its parts

With all the difficulties of figuring out how to walk together, why not just walk alone? You can window shop and take your time, stop for a cup of coffee when you get the urge, ponder the sky. One foot in front of the other, walking alone is so much simpler.

Why bend your schedule to sync with someone else's? Why go to bed later just to go out for dessert together? Why miss your favorite TV show to chat longer on the phone? Why bother? Why go through all the trouble to embrace another person?

Because sometimes walking with another can be so much more exciting than walking alone. Because walking with another you might discover things you wouldn't even imagine on your own. Because together we can create something bigger than just the two of us: something that is more than just the sum of its parts.

Tango is about a relationship in which 1+1 doesn't equal 2, but 1, says Rodolfo Dinzel.[6] This one entity has more potence than just the simple summation of each of its components; each part adds to the other.

So, if the company's good and you're enjoying the walk, why wouldn't you want to walk together? Sometimes the compromises are worth it. And only when they're worth it should you keep walking as one with another.

---

[6] As he wrote in his book, *El Tango, una danza: esa ansiosa búsqueda de la libertad,* Corregidor, Buenos Aires: 2008, p. 9.

Tango is a Good Friend

"Tango is a good friend," said Pepe.

And it's so true.

Tango is there when I need to celebrate life or lament heartache, on my good days and my not-so-good days. Tango helps me embrace people without questioning; to see them for who they are. Tango teaches me to embrace myself, too – the real me – and brings to light things I didn't even know about myself. I can't hide anything from Tango. Tango knows everything, even the things I don't say.

Embrace on a cold early-autumn night

After a long day of working at Bumbershoot with the chill early-autumn air nipping at every inch of my body, I took the 13 and another bus to the tunnel at Westlake where I caught the 71 to meet Terry at the Scarlet Tree. There was live music, but I was so exhausted that all I was good for was making the effort to hold my head up and prop myself up with a chair.

When I told him it was impossible, this guy coaxed me into dancing with him. We danced slow and smooth and at the end of the song, I thought I was done. But then Terry's friend came over and put his arms around me and leaned his face against mine and the warmth of his embrace melted the cold that had enveloped me. My body, my mind, and my heart surrendered; I felt the music through his movements and we danced.

Tango is about the connection

Dancing with Camilo Díaz one day, he told me to let go with my arms. As we spun around each other, he held me with his eyes. And I held on with mine.

The connection is more than just the physical act of wrapping yourself around another; it comes from the *mirada*[7], from your feet sharing a common surface, your mutual energy, the way you speak to each other without words, the way that nothing supercedes the intention of staying together, connected, each of you choosing to be one.

Connection is a choice and it takes the collaborative effort of both people. Having a bond with someone is more than just being physically present,[8] more than just an embrace. Two people can be far from each other and still be very much emotionally connected. Two people can be in each other's arms and not be connected at all.[9]

Tango is about the connection. Without the connection, you have nothing; with it, you have endless possibilities. That's why you can have amazing dances "just" walking, in impossibly tight spaces, with all levels of dancers. It's not about how long you've been dancing or how many moves you know – it's about sharing yourself with someone who understands you. That's why we keep coming back for more.

---

[7] *mirada* – gaze, eye contact before you dance (the *cabeceo*)

[8] "No es lo mismo ser que estar" by Alejandro Sanz cited by Rodolfo Dinzel, 2009.

[9] Horacio Godoy, March 10, 2011.

There's a lid for every pot

What a relationship looks like from the outside is not always indicative of how it feels on the inside.

I watched a tango performance in which it looked to me like the guy was rough and manhandling the woman – I didn't like the way he treated her. But they chose each other, so there must be something below the surface that works for them. Like my friend Débora says, *hay un roto para cada descosido* – there's a broken one for every unstitched one, or there's someone for everyone. What's fantastic for one person might not even make sense to another. And it's not up to anyone else to judge.

When we find a really good fit, when we find a pot for our lid, it doesn't really matter what anyone else thinks.

Life as a Four-Legged Animal

The Elastic Embrace

A relationship between two people needs to be stable enough to withstand the changes, yet fluid and elastic enough to allow each person to grow. It's about the strength of the bond rather than the physical strength of each individual. Although an oak tree (*el roble*) is stronger than a reed (*el junco*), the reed can better withstand the powerful winds of a storm – instead of fighting the wind, it sways with it. The relationship we look for in tango is a blend of consistency and flexibility, a bond that can be sustained while in motion.

Equilibrio de un Cuadrúpedo – Balancing as a Quadruped

In tango we go from our mere two-legged existence to being part of a four-legged creature. Our partner's legs are ours and vice versa. Together we establish a connection and together we manage our balance. If one leg falters a bit, we stabilize it using the other three – we collaborate.

A true four-legged animal should be able to trust all four of its legs, but we are accustomed to walking on two. To function as one creature, we need to develop trust in our partner's two legs, learning to rely on them just as we do our own. Our four-leggedness depends on our cohesiveness. It only works if we act as a team and grow to have faith in one another, especially when things get difficult. We need each other. And if we maintain the intention of solving our problems together, balance will not be an issue.

Since we're not really one creature, from time to time, we'll need to check in and readjust to make sure that we are both comfortable. We change throughout the dance. Each tango, each *tanda*,[10] each time we encounter one another, we need to take just a little time to calibrate and check in with our other half, even if we know each other very well. We are two dynamic creatures forming one quadruped.

[10] *tanda* – a set of 3-5 (usually 4) songs, which you generally dance with one partner

Bailar las Caídas[11] – Dance the Wobbles

En el tango no tenemos problemas de equilibrio
justo porque somos flexibles
como el junco enfrentándose al viento fuerte.
Bailamos las caídas, así nunca caemos.
No hay culpa si hay colaboración.
La rigidez contra el mundo,
contra nuestro compañero no sirve.
No nos peleamos con la realidad;
la bailamos.
Porque la idea es seguir juntos,
caminar y estar juntos,
manteniendo el abrazo de dos que forman uno.
Buscamos tierra, echamos raíces,
nos abrazamos y caminamos.

In tango, balance isn't an issue
precisely because we are flexible,
like reeds facing the strong winds of a storm.
We dance the wobbles, that way we never fall.
There is no blame in collaboration,
there's no sense in being rigid against our partner.
We don't fight our reality –
we dance it.
Because the objective is to continue together,
to walk and to be together,
maintaining our embrace of two who form one.
We seek the earth beneath our feet, set roots,
we embrace and walk.

---

[11] There is actually a move in tango called *la caída,* "the fall"; rather than fighting the momentum, you use it to produce another movement.

There will always be wobbles. They're part of life. If we get upset and start pointing fingers, we amplify them and it's a lot more work to synchronize again. The wobbles are as big or as small as we make them. We can fight them or we can dance them; dance the wobbles.

Sentido de flotación – A floating sensation

One of the first things I noticed when watching a room full of people dancing tango was that, even though all kinds of fancy things were happening below the waist, they looked like they were floating. Despite all the changes around them and their moving around the dance floor, there was consistency in their embraces. This little something, this energy they cultivated between them, was what allowed them to sustain their connection when they transcended the most difficult moments – it was what created the sensation that they were floating.

If we can develop and sustain a consistent bond with our partner, we can endure and embrace the challenges, the surprises, and the beauty of a life and a world and a dance floor and a union that is inevitably and constantly changing. Even with the world spinning dizzyingly around us, we can feel like we're floating.

Sweet Vulnerability

***Entregarse* – To give oneself**

Giving oneself, *entregarse,* involves trust. But trust is easier said than done, because our trust issues generally start and end with us.

Trusting involves taking risks. Since creating a connection takes two people, since you are so close to one another and leaning – albeit slightly – toward each other, sharing an axis, you depend on each other to make it work. You lean with the faith that your partner will meet you halfway.

And you can't hold back. You either commit or you don't, because if you go into a situation with your insecurities creating a wall before you, trying to prove him a poor candidate, he will be. If you intend to catch her in the act of letting you down, you will. He can't meet you halfway if you don't lean, too.

By facing your problems alone, you become stronger individually, but in order to strengthen a bond, you have to work together. The hard part is letting go and allowing someone to help when things get tough; if you surrender a little of yourself and commit to leaning toward your partner, you no longer have full control of the situation – neither of you do. But taking the risk that you might have to pick up the pieces on your own is the only way to truly build something with your partner; giving of yourself is the only way to really dance together.

Fear of falling

> "Regret for the things we did can be tempered by time; it is regret for the things we did not do that is inconsolable."
>
> – Sydney J. Harris

Well, the fact is that many of the men I've met in Argentina who dance tango are not that tall. Or maybe that's because I'm not that short. Either way, I end up being the same height or a bit taller in many of the combinations. When a friend asked me to stand in for his partner in a dance group, I was excited about the opportunity to perform and eagerly accepted. I am bigger than him and taller when in heels. That's just the way it is. We had danced before, but when we took it up a notch practicing in the studio one day – wild energy, dips and things – I felt uncomfortable. I would arch back for a dip and stop myself midway.

Ana Ventura noticed. She said, "Great things come out while you guys play, but you keep stopping yourself, like you're not completely committing to the movement."

"I'm afraid to fall," I admitted.

"Let go," she said. "Go for it."

"But what if I fall?"

"Vivir toda la vida así? – Live your whole life like this? So you fall once or twice and then you won't fall anymore. It's better than always stopping yourself halfway."

She was right. I knew she was. Sometimes it just takes someone else to tell you. Her words gave me the courage to let go and commit to the more "risky" movements. Once I stopped fearing myself, I was able to connect better with my partner and it turned out not to be so scary after all.

If you search for security over happiness, the second will be the price you'll have to pay for the first.[12] Nothing good comes without some risk. It's better to try and fail than to live in fear of not doing it "right," without ever really taking any leaps, without ever really experiencing life, with the anxiety and regret of having never tried at all.

[12] My translation of a Spanish translation of Richard Bach's quote: "Shop for security over happiness and we buy it, at that price."

An act of faith

Tango is an act of faith, says Rodolfo Dinzel, because we don't know where we'll end up or what the path will look like, but we trust that we want to journey this tango together.

When we're young, not knowing means adventure and opportunity. But as we grow up and learn about the range of terrible possibilities, the unknown begins to generate fear. Surrendering ourselves to our emotions, to our partner, to the moment, not knowing what will happen along the road – that's scary.

Life is full of unknowns. It comes with no roadmap; you'll find no checkpoints. And relationships with those that surround us are mysterious and fluid and guarantee nothing. They can inspire us to be better than we ever thought we could be – for a day, a week, a lifetime. They are completely improvised and unpredictable. And that is precisely what makes them so beautiful: in embarking upon a path not taken, in not knowing what the adventure will entail, we leave ourselves open to so many possibilities, to the probability that things will unfold in a way that we could not even have imagined.

Links to people are fleeting. We don't know how many tangos we have left. We don't know whether a prelude to a kiss will at some point lead to a kiss; that's what makes the prelude so enticing.

When we realize that the unknown is what allows life to surprise us, we begin to relish these little moments. We don't know where we're going or how we'll get there or what our journey during the next 3-minute tango will entail. What I do know is that I commit to dancing this next tango with you and trust that you and I can embrace and move across the floor and create something transient and fleeting and beautiful together.

It feels better to kiss someone when they kiss you back

Since giving involves making yourself vulnerable, it feels better to give when your partner does so, too, or at least when they're open to receiving what you're giving.

"Each force is answered by an equal and opposite reaction," explained my high school physics teacher, "Try this over spring break: kiss someone and see if they kiss you back." He was laughing so hard that he could hardly get the words out, but he was right: it's nice to kiss someone when they return your kiss with proportionate force. If the force is very disproportionate – they pull away or smother you – things can become a little uncomfortable.

It feels nice if someone accepts when you offer the most important thing you have to offer: yourself. It feels better to kiss someone when they kiss you back.

Take* like you mean it

En una pareja, hay que saber ofrecer. En vez de empujar o esforzar, hay que saber ofrecer la oportunidad para que la otra persona pueda decidir tomar lo ofrecido por su propia voluntad. Ofrecer sin dudas, sin prejuicios, sin miedos – así el otro se siente seguro de lo que quieres y lo que ofreces. Y hay que saber tomar y tomar con ganas, porque si no, el ofrecer ya no tiene mucho sentido.

In a relationship, you have to know how to give. Instead of pushing or forcing, provide the opportunity for your partner to decide to take what you are offering of her own will.

Give like you mean it – without doubts, without prejudgments, without hesitation. That way, your partner can be clear about what you want and what it is you are offering.

And you have to know how to take wholeheartedly and without reservation, without apprehension or fear, because otherwise, offering loses its meaning.

* I chose to use the word "take" rather than "accept" or "receive" because it's ok to take something – not grab or snatch or steal, but take. You don't have to be passive and timid and wait for it to be placed in your hand. If you want something someone is offering, take it. If they don't want to give it to you, they shouldn't offer.

When you want more, give more

Trust is a lot to ask of someone, especially when they are struggling with it. Instead of scolding someone who is hesitant to trust – which will likely cause them to withdraw that much more into their shell – ask yourself: What is it he fears? How can I help ease that tension?

When you want more than someone is giving, start by giving more yourself. Angela Sarmiento once told me, "I give a lot of myself in my dance and I hope that my partner will do the same." She did. I could feel it. When we danced, she gave so openly and, without expecting anything, encouraged me to do the same. She took a risk and that made me feel more comfortable giving more of myself, too.

Whereas demands and expectations provoke defensive impulses to draw back, for every nice gesture, for every kind word, people feel compelled to return the favor – it makes them also want to give. When people offer themselves of their own will, they are happier about it and usually the person receiving is happier, too.

Let me share myself with you

Wrap yourself around me and make me feel like you want to hold me, for a few tangos.

You want to get a little closer? Even better. But remember, you're strong, so please keep in mind that there's a person in your arms, that this person needs to breathe, that I have flesh and body parts that all need space to be here and maybe space to readjust sometimes.

Instead of pulling me in with your sheer strength, try giving me a little more. Don't keep all that "good stuff" to yourself, as Michelle Badion says; share it with me. Think about what you can do with your own body to decrease the distance between us. Make it easier for me to approach you. When you focus on what I'm not giving you, you actually make it harder for me to give to you. And if I'm not comfortable getting closer, meet me where I'm at. Sometimes I just need a little space; let me choose what's comfortable for me.

There's power in offering and power in taking. I accepted your invitation to dance and I am still here asking for more in every moment we spend together. What you can do is make my choice easier or more attractive, but you can't make it for me, nor do you really want to. Let me connect with you, let me choose you, let me share myself with you.

Light as a feather, stiff as a board

November 15, 2010

> While dancing with a friend who is much smaller than me at the studio today, I noticed that whenever I felt my balance compromised, I pulled on him and caved my chest in. This reflex reaction put a strain on him as he had to compensate. Rather than working with him, I was just taking care of myself. Thinking back to a conversation about posture with Rodolfo Dinzel, I realized that my approach was counterproductive for our partnership. So I decided to try giving myself more willingly, to trust, *entregarme.* With this shift of energy toward him rather than away from him, balance became much easier and our dance became more fluid.

Although he is significantly smaller than me in size, he has the power of a lion. Nonetheless I hesitated: If I leaned toward him, would he be able to support me? If only he could provide me with the security I needed from him – which I had already decided he couldn't give me – to compensate for my insecurity in myself. It wasn't really about whether he was strong enough; my fear was that I would cause us to fall.

If what I wanted from him was more support, I needed to give him more, too. That's where my fear got in the way. Like the light as a feather, stiff as a board exercise, the more you trust yourself, the easier it is for your partner to hold you up and be there for you. If you hold back, your partner's job becomes more difficult. When I tried trusting him to support me, when I took a risk and compromised my balance in order to really enter into the relationship of a shared axis, when I depended on him, it turned out to be nothing like what I had feared. The more we danced, the more comfortable I got with the situation, with him, with myself.

We often hold back and hide behind our prejudgments. While it's easy to see how a problem might have to do with my partner – he's much taller, much shorter, half my weight, divorced, has kids, etc. – the real challenge is overcoming my own fears, which have more to do with me than with my partner.

Meeting Myself Where I'm At

Breathe

February 22, 2011

It's been years since I stopped breathing. I mean really breathing. It's like at some point, I stopped really taking the air into my lungs, letting it seep into my cells and tingle my skin. I just do the superficial, just what's necessary to survive. Breathe in. Breathe out.

I've started taking cold showers – at first because I liked how it woke up my skin and made me aware of the surface of my body and now because the hot water knob seems to be stuck and all I can get from the shower is cold water. No matter how hot it is outside, the cold water is always a shock to my system. My initial reflex reaction is to cringe, hold my breath, and tighten all the muscles I can to prepare for the ensuing attack. But what I try to get my body to do instead is release. Release, exhale, relax, and breathe.

And now that I'm conscious of it, I catch myself stopping my breath in daily activities. Writing the previous sentence, for example. I was so concentrated on getting my thought on paper before I forgot or before the next cascade of ideas came barreling at me, that I caught myself not breathing – neither in nor out.

So my strategy is this: I'm trying to be more aware of my breathing. Consistent and deep rather than that on-the-surface shallow, letting the oxygen seep into my cells by opening them to receive it. In order to retrain (because this is a natural process I have learned to impede) myself to open my cells to be irrigated by this life-sustaining, fueling substance, I need to breathe out and make space for the fresh air to come in. In order to receive the new, I have to clean out some of the old and make space in my closet, my daily calendar, my mind. In order to breathe in, I have to breathe out.

Dancing tango helps me remember to relax and to breathe. The more I relax, the more I can feel my partner and the faster I can respond to his movements because my body just goes with him instinctively. In order to receive this time-sensitive, in-the-moment information from him, I can't hold onto the old and can't fill my mind with thoughts of the last technique class I took – I just have to release and be and give of myself so that I can receive what he's offering me. Try it the next time you go to embrace someone on the dance floor: take a big breath and exhale it all out, relax and connect with the floor. Then you'll be ready to feel the pulse of his movements, to listen, to perceive his suggestions and his invitations, to receive his breath and give him yours.

Note: Embracing to dance a tango generally implies embarking upon a journey into the unknown. Learning to relax in the face of the unknown is no easy task; some say it's a lifelong journey.

A Reflection of Myself

The leaves change colors, flowers bloom, things get rusty and old, dew drops roll off flower petals, babies start pulling themselves up by holding onto things and soon they're walking on their own. It's easier to observe the transformations in others, to notice their patterns. Since we live with ourselves all the time, the gradual changes in us can be less palpable, so subtle sometimes that we completely fail to perceive them.

The choices we make about who we relate with have to do with something within us, with an energy we consciously or unconsciously seek out. Each person we dance with, each person we choose to interact with reflects a different facet of ourselves back at us; they capture in their particular angle of light a tiny part of us and mirror it. Sometimes the things we notice in others are actually our own issues reflected back at us. Recognizing this can help us understand ourselves.

We don't exist in a vacuum. We are defined by our interactions with others. If a tree falls in the woods and no one is around to hear it, does it make a sound? And if no one is there to hear it, does it even matter? We are because of our relationship with the world that surrounds us, because of our contact with others.

It's as if sometimes we lose sight of ourselves; we become invisible. And a simple touch can bring us back. Our existence is reaffirmed with each embrace we share. We all need this exchange, because we constantly lose and find ourselves – it's an on-going process we have to keep working at.

Integrity and Individual Limits: Meeting Myself Where I'm At

Most of us don't come with an instruction manual and for those of us that do, there are amendments upon amendments. We figure out our limits as we go. It's a lifelong dance between the me I wish I was, the me people think I should be, the me I think people think I should be, and the me I really am.

But this is not a game of "mercy" – we don't come to the *milonga* or live life to see how much pain we can endure – it's not a contest to see who gives up first. Some pains help you grow – they're usually the ones you have no choice about. Other pains are a result of the choices you make because of what you think you need at the time. And then there are those pains that you can avoid, or better yet, work through to make them go away. Why live with unnecessary pain?

Not until recently did I stop fighting myself; it's one of my newest amendments. I found myself in a place where I couldn't find my place. Between here and there and back and forth, I somehow ended up in the back room, putting on my high-heeled shoes. One shoe, to be specific. And, without even having buckled my silver shoe, I looked at the other shoe and had to ask myself, "Self, do you really want to put on this other shoe?" And I had a quick exchange between me and myself, asking whether putting on the other shoe was an act of my free will because what I wanted was to stay, or was it because I thought I should stay, or that others might think I should stay. What did *I* really want was the question: to put on the other shoe or not to put on the other shoe? And every inch of me participated in taking off that first shoe. I gathered my things and without another thought about what I *should* do, I decided to do what I felt.

If you choose to keep bending over backwards, people will think that it's normal for you, and you can't blame your back pain on someone else. If it hurts or you're uncomfortable, change something. We can't expect people to know what we need; it's unreasonable. Not to mention that they can't read our minds, our needs change as we do. Although to us it might seem all too clear that someone's action is causing us pain, people don't always realize when they hurt us. Take care of you, and I mean this in the best, most selfless way. If you know what you need, things will be much easier for those around you. This is not individualism or egocentrism; it's clarity.

In tango, because women are often conditioned to "let go," to surrender themselves, it's really crucial to find ourselves again. I caught myself becoming bitter that my partner was pushing me onto my heel and then asking me to turn. Don't fight, but do show him what you need. What you really want might not always seem so clear to you, but you know what's good for you. That's why your hand hurts when you touch a hot pan fresh out of the oven, why you yawn when you partied all night long, why your stomach hurts if you're hungry, and that's why I hesitated to put on the other shoe.

You have the liberty of adding more amendments as you see fit. Be honest in your actions, your movements in the dance, and your partner will know. And that includes everything from not doing the *gancho*[13] he obviously wants if you don't feel comfortable or safe, to asking him to wait if you're not ready for the next move, to saying "thank you"[14] and "no" when that's what you feel, and saying "yes" only when you really want to.

---

[13] *gancho* – a movement that involves "hooking" your leg around your partner

[14] Saying "thank you" on the dance floor in tango generally means that you are done dancing with that person for the time being or for the rest of the evening.

It's a negotiation

You want this?

Well, I can give you that.

And you work from there. Sometimes it's smoother and other times it takes a little more wiggling and playing with the numbers to make it work. It's about finding a middle ground between what you each want and need and what you can offer one another. It's a compromise to find a way to meet each other where you're at.

Take Care of You

Maintain your own axis

Pull your own weight, or in tango, maintain your own axis, which does not mean that you don't give yourself to and share an axis with your partner. We're good with extremes, but working that middle ground between being so independent that we become withdrawn and rigid and being so open and giving and loose and undefined that we fall onto our partner and lose ourselves, that's the tricky part. Equality and partnership is about finding the strength not to let our fears get the best of us, about sharing, giving, finding that delicate balance of being independent and dependent, reliable and relying at the same time.

If your partner walks away, theoretically, you shouldn't fall. The idea is that you depend on each other not because you can't stand on your own, but because you want to be connected. Even though there shouldn't be a need to stand independently, you should never become so dependent on your partner that you cease to exist on your own or stop doing your part in the relationship. There's a difference between being needy and being present. As Mariana Dragone says, "I want to go with him, but I stay in my body. *No le peso* – I don't burden or weigh him down."

It's not unreasonable to trust that your partner will be there, since you agreed to dance together and the point isn't for him to jump away and say, "Aha! You fell!" In a dynamic situation where the terrain is constantly changing, there will be times when you lean more toward him and times when he leans more toward you. You have to adapt and help each other. The idea is to do your part not to overburden him by letting your body be too loose or too tense and not to push or pull him downward.

When we embrace with another to dance a tango, we are not looking for a sad puppy to carry around or someone to babysit or compensate for. We seek an encounter with a person who will be strong enough to stand on his or her own and strong enough to participate and share and make up half of the whole we create together.

Your Issues or My Issues?

Take care of you, not just for yourself, but for your partner, too. When you are on edge or stressed out, if you are constantly testing yourself, the people you interact with will likely feel the anxiety of being tested, too. If you are afraid to fail, you transmit this tension to your partner. We often project our issues onto others without even realizing it. We do it so much, in fact, that sometimes we convince ourselves that our problems are actually our partner's.

If I can learn to accept myself as I am, I will be able to do the same with the people around me. If I am whole, I have more to share with my partner.

Make Space for Yourself

When it comes to our own individual space, we have all probably had the sensation that things might be easier in this dance if we took up less space – the *giros*, the *ochos,*[15] we could maneuver. The fact is that many, many of us do take up too much space, and it has nothing to do with that extra *medialuna* you grabbed for breakfast at La Viruta[16] last night or the fact that some of us have larger hips than others. Many of us take up more space than our natural body make-up would require due to our poor posture.

Who hasn't heard a teacher say, don't look at your feet! Keep your head up! And we obediently lift our heads for just a minute before sinking into the same inclination to look at what marvelous things are happening with our feet. But one day, I heard Olga Besio say, "If you look down, you're taking someone else's space." How obvious! If my head is not aligned on top of my spine and I'm hunched over, I am taking someone else's space: my partner's.

Mariana Dragone says, our hips stick out and head moves forward because we don't make room for them in the vertical alignment of our spinal column. If I stretch my heels toward the floor and the top of my head toward the ceiling, lengthening my spinal column from top to bottom (from my tailbone to the top of my head), my hips and neck and everything else all of a sudden have space to arrange themselves comfortably. Try it. Even if you're sitting, you can stretch just your spine. You'll notice right away that your posture improves.

---

[15] *giros* – turns; *ochos* – spiral movements that look like a figure 8

[16] A tango club/milonga in Buenos Aires where they serve *medialunas* (half moon-shaped pastries) for breakfast at 4:30am on the weekends.

Al poner el carrito en marcha, los melones se acomodan solos – you don't have to worry about arranging the melons, because once you get the cart moving, they arrange themselves. This saying reminds me of an email chain I received about the golf balls, sand, and coffee in a jar analogy. Basically, there's always space to fit in the small stuff once you get the important things in order. If you put the sand in first, there isn't room for the golf balls. If I focus on my priorities – health, family, friends, career, etc. – the details will fall into place. When I don't lengthen my spinal column, that's when things get pushed out of the way and have to find space for themselves. When I do lengthen my spine and make room for all of me, everything has space to align. I can actually get in the way of someone getting closer to me; I can get in the way of my own dreams. In making room for myself, I in turn, make room for my partner.

Good posture isn't just good; it's essential

Good posture isn't just good; it's essential. Be it because I'm insecure or unsure of where my feet are, just like in a relationship, it's unfair to ask my partner to compensate for my insecurities or for me to take them out on another person instead of dealing with my issues myself.

If you can't help but hunch over, ok, but let your partner choose how close they get. One huge tip: don't pull anyone closer than they want to be. They have their reasons or they'd be closer to you – they might be her issues or yours, or a mix, but don't force it. We all have reasons for keeping our distance.

One night at La Glorieta, an outdoor *milonga* in Belgrano, Buenos Aires, I embraced with a nice older gentleman to dance a tango. It quickly became apparent to me that there was something about the way he held his back that did not mesh well with how I wanted to hold mine. I tried to push away a little to give myself space to come out of the front *ochos* he was leading, but he counteracted my efforts by tightening his right arm. This lasted one tango and I was not comfortable with continuing the game, so I asked him for what I needed: a bit looser on the grip, please. I followed my request up with a smile and "I promise I won't do anything crazy."

"And you won't run away?"

"Nope. I decided to dance with you and I'm not going anywhere."

Instead of fighting each other, we spent the rest of the *tanda* playing and dancing.

Why are you pinching my hand?

I've been struggling with myself over my anxiety around the negative. Expressing anything that could possibly be seen as negative, or rather, that I see as negative, makes me anxious, because I know that my Scorpio sting is one of my flaws. For years I've tried to quietly acquiesce and avoid confrontation, but that usually leads to my becoming resentful, which is even worse. I'm a work in progress.

The other night, I was dancing with a guy who kept squeezing my right hand.[17] Common, yet not comfortable. So, I tried to ask him subtly for the change I needed by showing him, stretching my fingers out sideways and making space for them before readjusting my contact with his hand. Once. Twice. Three times. As soon as I relaxed my hand, he'd squeeze it again.

We chatted between tangos, but I remember little of what we talked about because I was still upset about my hand. The next tango began and this time I took what I saw as a more direct approach: I squeezed his hand, too. This he noticed right away.

"Why are you pinching my hand?" he asked, taken aback.

"You were squeezing mine and it hurt."

"So you take revenge?" Well, I hadn't seen it that way, but I guess that is exactly what I was doing. "Why didn't you just tell me?"

I started to explain that I had tried to communicate by showing him… but I realized that that didn't really matter. Obviously, the message that seemed loud and clear to me was not so to him. I guess I wasn't sure how he'd take it.

---

[17] on the open side of the embrace – the side where your hands meet

What I actually did was assume that he would not be receptive to my verbal request to let up on his grip. Without giving him the chance to decide how to react, I assumed the worst. And when he confronted me about my passive-aggressive methods, I really had little to say in my defense. He squeezed less in the next two dances and we ended the *tanda* peacefully.

It's true that not all men take a comment that your spine hurts or that you can't breathe or could you please use a little less force, well. But there really is little reason not to try – with a smile and good intentions – to communicate your needs. If you can't find a middle ground or a comfortable modification or your partner becomes angry and turns into a fire-breathing monster, then maybe you shouldn't continue dancing together anyway. There's really no good reason to suffer if you feel uncomfortable nor to dance with someone who doesn't care enough about your comfort to try to accommodate your needs. Life is too short.

I know that you don't mean to hurt me, but…

I had a conversation with a friend the other day about separating what someone is saying or doing from their intention in doing it – separating the action from the intention. Or rather, when analyzing an action, taking into consideration the intention with which it was produced. So, if you know the circumstances around say, an offensive or rude remark, you should not get as upset about it.

Although I can agree that there is a difference between insulting someone because your intention is to hurt their feelings and insulting someone without intending to do so or because that's all you know, there comes a point when you have to take responsibility for not only the intention with which you do things, but also for the way they come out and the consequences they provoke. Healthy interactions with people have healthy and real limits. I understand that you're having a bad day, but if you don't look up when you're walking and bump into me, it still hurts.

In the case of the tango embrace, let's assume that the intentions are good (if not, we have a different caliber of problem). Even with the best intentions, if someone hunches over while squeezing my spine toward him in a manner that causes me to contort my body and hurt my back and neck (and other cascading effects), it is not acceptable. It is mistreatment and a lack of respect for the other person's body, knowingly or unknowingly. No one goes to a *milonga* to hurt people (at least not these days – no more *arma blanca* and *malevos* and *guapos*),[18] just as no one goes to a *milonga* to suffer.

---

[18] a reference to the gangster/mafia culture that was once associated with some people in the tango realm

One *tanda,* I felt uncomfortable and hesitantly asked the man I was dancing with to please use a little less force. I was pleasantly surprised by his response: "*Gracias,*" he said, "*Cualquier hombre que no lo quiera escuchar es un pelotudo y no debería bailar con vos* – Any man who doesn't want to hear it is a jerk and doesn't deserve to dance with you."

Just because someone doesn't mean to hurt you doesn't mean it doesn't hurt. When we stop excusing pain or putting our pride first, we can start dealing with the issue: I'm hurting, not because you want to hurt me, but I feel pain nonetheless. It's not an attack on you, but a statement about me and my needs. It's not about proving who's right or wrong; it's about finding a way to make the relationship work for both of us.

Dancing to the Beat of Our Souls

La rubiecita – The blonde

I had been working a lot on my posture as a lead, on not crowding my partner and not invading her space in the embrace by letting my left arm (on the open side) drop forward. But when the tango ended, she remarked, "I feel like your arm is too far away, like I have to reach for it." Not only was I surprised to hear this, but I could think of a variety of reasons why my arm might feel far away – her head forward, her right arm too far back with her elbow dropped, the fact that she wasn't facing me…

As I stood there composing my response, I suddenly realized that none of those supposedly technically-correct elements matter. The fact is that each person I dance with is different. If it makes her feel more comfortable for me to let my left arm come forward, I should adapt to her structure, just as she must do with mine, so that we can compromise and form one entity for the duration of the tangos we dance. My job is to make my partner feel comfortable, and that supercedes any rulebook.

We dance with people, not theoretical models. The key is to become skilled at perceiving the needs of each person and learn to adapt to the reality that each partner provides, because each person and each tango we dance with each person, is different.

Moving to his beat

Arms around his neck, his hands on my hips, swaying from side to side.[19] The beat was definitely not the same in his ears as in mine.

And at some point, I decided that if he was a little off the beat I heard, it didn't really matter that much to me. If I could move to his beat, if I could breathe with him and blend with him, being with him was more important than fighting the battle of who was right and who was wrong or forcing ourselves to march to anyone else's beat. Sometimes we get so caught up in the way things "should" be, the patterns of society, our plans, what others think, that we lose sight of the beauty of the way things are. We forget the importance of really listening to one another and start talking at each other. The beat = what "should" be, and the feeling of our bodies swaying from side to side = what is.

And if I don't respect the person I'm dancing with enough to put the music and the beat second to his and our needs, why am I dancing with him, anyway? Sometimes the only thing that matters is that you feel where your partner is and let him know where you are. Move as one and you can find a way to work from there, embracing the reality of what you both bring to the table.

So when I catch myself confusing my priorities and anxious about respecting the beat, I remind myself that if I'm not connected with my partner, I'm dancing alone, to my beat or someone else's, but dancing alone.

I wrap my arms around him just a little tighter and breathe out so I can synchronize with him. I start matching the undulations of his body, and we dance to the rhythm of our souls.

---

[19] This wasn't tango, but having worked so much on connecting with my partner gave me a different perspective.

Anyone can dance with a really advanced dancer

After one of her Wednesday technique classes, Anita Postorino told me, "Anyone can dance with a really advanced dancer"; but not just anyone can dance with someone who is less advanced than them. You have to compensate and be patient and listen very attentively. And you have to remember that things that come easily to you (now that you've been practicing them for a while) might be easier said than done to someone else.

It's easy to see the flaws in your partner – he[20] leans too far over and pushes me onto my heel, he doesn't leave space for me to enter into the forward *ocho*, he doesn't wash the dishes, take out the trash, he this, he that – but it's much harder to see yourself. Instead of being frustrated that one guy doesn't dance me the same way another one does, I can be more proactive. If he doesn't make enough space for me, I can gently show him where I need it. If I let him push my weight onto my heels, I push back just a little so that I can get back to the balls of my feet. Tell him where you are, ask for what you need. It's not fair to put the responsibility on one person's shoulders. Give him a chance. Don't give up on him.

Anyone can dance with a really advanced dancer because you don't have to compensate or accommodate much. Learning to stay humble while you adapt and patiently give of yourself is more difficult. Being patient is not easy – with others and maybe even more so, with yourself.

---

[20] My use of **gender-specific pronouns,** "he" for leads and "she" for follows, respectively, is for the purpose of convenience and clarity, not meant to negate the fact that both men and women can lead and follow and sometimes it doesn't even matter who's doing what because it flows. In general, they can be used interchangeably. Please substitute what makes sense for you.

Dance for your partner

You can tell when your partner is dancing for you, when he's listening to you and waiting for you to get to a point at which you're ready for the next step instead of rushing you or beating you there, when she's paying attention to what you want to tell her, when you take precedence over her latest embellishments.[21] You can tell when your partner is so into him or herself that you come second. You can tell if your partner is dancing for you or for those watching, when it's more about appearances than about how you feel.

Olga Besio observes, *"Muchos hombres están mirando por afuera. No esperan a la mujer y les queda en la axila* – Many men are looking outside. They don't wait for the woman and she ends up in their armpit." Try to be conscious of where your partner is and what your partner needs from you. Pay attention to her axis; give her time to complete each move before asking her for the next step. She'll feel more comfortable, and since her axis is part of your shared (quadruped) axis, you'll feel better, too. *"Si vamos a bailar, bailás conmigo,"* Olga Besio says to tell the guys – "If we're going to dance, dance with me."

In tango, you ask a lot of each other. You ask that your partner lean toward you and trust you to be there. The more stable and consistent you are, the more confident your partner will feel. On your own, you can fall down and brush yourself off, but in a union it's no longer just about how resilient you are and how quickly you can bounce back. It's about both of you. If you fall, you run the risk of letting your partner down, too. A union means added benefits, but it also brings some extra responsibilities and extra

---

[21] embellishments or adornments – stylistic touches one can add to the dance

motivation to keep it together. It means that if you let yourself fall apart, your partner will be affected, too. Work together to move together; it doesn't matter who gets there first.

Appreciate Your Partner

Knowing what it feels like to do what it is you are asking of your partner can help you empathize and be more patient. It can help you be a more sensitive lead and a more present follow. Put yourself in the other person's shoes: What does she need from you in order to do what you are asking? What does it feel like to walk backwards and trust another person to keep you out of harm's way? What's it like to try to protect your partner and make her feel comfortable and entertained all at the same time? What does it feel like to dance with you?

Relaxing is Work, Too

If you're more experienced at something, it can be easy to forget what it was like to learn as a beginner. Big problems seem like easy fixes because you already know what you know, but learning and incorporating new concepts into your body is a gradual process. You get frustrated with someone who is already sweating bullets trying to remember the long list of new things to work on all at the same time.

And it's normal – on both ends – to collide in this situation. The person who's more experienced gets frustrated because it feels that they're not asking a lot, while the person who's less experienced feels like they're trying and working hard and still it's not enough.

Problems between two people never go one way. It's never one person's fault, even if you "know what you're doing," even if your role is more dominant, even if you are the one "teaching." When we come at our issues with an angle of who's right and who's wrong, we miss the point: that collaboration takes both of us and that we have a problem to resolve, together.

Keep perspective. The less experienced dancer might look for strategies to help her work through the issue, while the person with more experience should keep in mind that change takes time.

Even relaxing, which sounds easy enough, takes work. If what you're looking for in your partner is for her to relax, see what you can do in your body to help. Depending on the context, ask your partner what she needs, or try to sense it by paying attention to when your partner seems to tense up the most. Breathe, try to relax yourself – it can be contagious – and remember that relaxing is work, too.

Make Him Feel Good About Himself

Let him think he's making the decisions, controlling the situation. The man is the head of the household, but the woman is the neck. And why not? You need both a head and a neck to function. So let your man make some decisions, control some things – encourage him to take the initiative. Give him tools to be successful; help build him up.

And be as subtle as possible. We all like to feel successful. We like it much more when we feel like we had something to do with our own success. There's no need to make it too obvious, to have your partner feel like you're doing a lot of work. Just give him a little push and reinforcement and let him take it from there.

"No nos sirve, mujeres, hacer que el hombre quede mal. Hay que hacer que el hombre quede bien," says Anita Postorino – "It doesn't help us, ladies, to make the man look bad. Make him look good." Make him look good and feel good, dance not just for yourself but for him, for this person who sought your embrace. The better you make him feel about himself, the better he'll feel about dancing with you. The really good dancers are the ones who make their partner feel like a really good dancer.

On a crowded dance floor, let him find solace in your embrace

When your partner is stressed out about navigating the constantly changing, crowded floor, is there anything you can do to help? Remember, he's not only trying to navigate the dance floor, but is also focused on you, the woman in his arms, and how to give you a fantastic dancing experience. Stay calm and be patient. Be extra attentive to his changes of direction. Try to make his job easier. Use your energy to soothe him and help him feel like the fancy steps don't always matter, and he might just gain more courage to play.

This is when you can really turn your attention inward, to the inner dance – the dance in the intimacy of the space your bodies share, with nuances imperceptible from the outside – that part of the dance that happens just between the two of you. Work the "inner space"[22] and he'll feel like all that you want from him is all that he is and what he has to offer you. He'll be able to relax and face the challenges of the turmoil around you, confident that between you two there is a connection. He'll feel like he is your focus, too, and that in itself is empowering.

When your significant other is going through a particularly tumultuous time, see if you can help by providing that safety of a familiar, consistent anchor. Let him know that the chaos around him doesn't have to invade the space between you two – the inner space. In the midst of all the uncertainties of life or the chaos of a crowded dance floor, let him find solace in your embrace.

---

[22] The idea of the inner and outer space in tango was introduced to me by Stefan Barth, March, 2010.

Life is good when the women in my life are happy

Sitting at the bar at the T.G.I. Friday's at the Atlanta airport on my way back to Buenos Aires for the second time, sipping on one of my beloved mudslides (we have a special relationship that goes back to Spiderman and Philly and UW with the ladies), the man next to me and I somehow end up immersed in conversation. He begins telling me about how he does things like play bartender for his wife and her friends for their ladies' get-togethers. He says he's happy to do it, because "life is good when my wife and the women in my life are happy."

We're all happier when we are all happier, because happiness is contagious. Don't worry about the steps. Figure out how to make her happy, be it just for a few tangos. Make her feel like the queen she is, like being in her presence is an honor. If she feels like she's dancing well, you'll sense it in her movements and you'll be able to play more together.

His confidence in me gave me confidence in myself

I had been dancing less than a year when my friend Alan Forte asked me to perform with him at a small *milonga* in Villa Urquiza. My initial response was "yes," but when we started practicing the nerves took over. I asked him several times if he was sure – he could change partners; I wouldn't be upset.

No, no, and finally he asked, You don't trust me?

I was shocked: Of course I trust you!

Well, I picked you and I'm not changing partners.

Wow. All of my anxiety with myself disappeared. Alan's confidence in me gave me confidence in myself.

Fear Paralyzes

Unless you are rebelling in rage and trying furiously to prove someone wrong, fear paralyzes. I'm not sure I want to create or be around that kind of energy. So, instead of pointing out all the flaws (and there will always be some to point out), try making constructive suggestions and celebrating the positives. Build the person up and they'll flourish.

When people feel good about themselves, they perform better all around. When they are less self-conscious, they're less inhibited. Sometimes all you need is to think you can do something and you're halfway there. Play his strengths, make her feel good about herself – the point isn't to show your partner that you know more than they do; the point is to connect with them.

Positivity goes a long way

This guy asked me to dance and when he started shuffling back and forth, I tried to guide him into more defined movements that I could work with as a follow. By the second tango he seemed to gain some confidence and by the third I noticed that when he went into certain sequences, his movements were more defined. I thought back to how Rodolfo Dinzel focuses on the positive aspects of his students' dance and how good it feels to get compliments about my own dance. I was so excited to have found something to compliment my partner on.

When we stopped dancing, I told him that I could feel the importance of his movements during certain sequences and it felt really good.

His face lit up. What a powerful tool positive encouragement is. As we parted ways, I could feel a different energy.

Speak Without Words

A new language

After the first Introduction to Tango Workshop I taught on Sunday, June 6, 2010, one of the people in attendance commented:

> "Enjoyed the connection exercises in the beginning. Connecting while closer, interestingly, was more difficult than when apart."

My response:

Tango is learning to speak without words, learning to communicate with our bodies in a way that many of us are not used to. Like any new language, when we first start speaking, it might feel awkward; we're cautious about the words we choose to express our ideas as we try to piece together coherent sentences. Yet this caution not to misrepresent our thoughts can actually impede our communication. As we develop the ability to communicate in this new language, it feels more and more comfortable and walking while holding each other closer becomes more fluid. As we incorporate this manner of transmitting signals to each other in our bodies, it becomes easier to speak without words.

What men think

Here's the big secret: we women might think we know what you're thinking, we might analyze and overanalyze, but really, we don't know. We don't know if you meant to call and got busy at work, if you miss us, if you want to see us, until you do something to indicate it. And every time I start trying to read someone's mind – I call it putting myself in "his" shoes – I have to remind myself that I can't. What you see is what you get.

And that's ok: we don't need to know everything you're thinking – it takes away from your autonomous decision to speak your mind and make your intentions known. It takes away from the intrigue of surprise. It's so nice when a man takes initiative.

Since we ladies can't read your mind, we don't know what you want until you ask for it, until you do it, until you invite us to come along. Not until you indicate the forward *ocho*, do we know that that is what you want. Until you do so, you have all the freedom to change course.

So if a move doesn't come out just the way you planned, don't worry about it. Part of the *tanguero canchero* attitude[23] is playing a little game of self-confidence. Even if you're not sure, play the role. Decide and commit to each movement. Add in some dramatic pauses. Envision getting there and you're halfway there already.

And if you make a "mistake,"[24] unless you step on your partner, knock over a table, or hit someone else, pretend it's what you meant to do. No one knows what you're thinking, and we women can't read your mind. Just fake it till you make it.[25]

---

[23] swagger: *tanguero* – a person who dances tango; *canchero* – cool
[24] How can there even be "mistakes" in an improvised dance, anyway?
[25] Marisa Mancke says this to motivate us in step aerobics class.

Tango is a conversation

In tango we speak to each other. It's a dialogue (*di* = "two") to which both people contribute. "50-50," says Eric Dinzel, referring to his parents' *Método Dinzel* – the Dinzel Method.[26] Even if you aren't the one talking, you are present and listening and nodding your head. Part of making sure it's not a monologue is being an active listener.

How you participate is different in each conversation. Olga Besio explains while we chat, *"A veces quieres proponer más, a veces quieres obedecer más* – Sometimes you want to propose more, sometimes you want to obey more." One day you might feel like talking a lot, another day you might feel like listening and just spicing up what his body says to you. Your dance is different depending on who you dance with and how you feel at each particular moment. Just as you wouldn't have the same conversation with your lover as with a child or a coworker, it doesn't make sense to have the same conversation with each person you dance with.

You might encounter people who just really love to talk, people who don't like to be interrupted. They're so captivated by their own conversation that they might even keep on talking if you were to walk away. These are the people whose idea of a conversation is more like a monologue. I, personally, like to participate actively in most conversations. But once in a while, I'll come across someone who likes to hear himself talk and if he's eloquent and his speech is really moving, I'll stay and listen, because I might learn something and because once in a while, it's nice. When I feel like I've heard all he has to say or all I

---

[26] Gloria and Rodolfo Dinzel's *Método Dinzel*

want to hear, I'll move on to a situation in which I can also share.

And then there are those rare times when you understand each other so well that you finish each other's sentences, build ideas together, elaborate on each other's thoughts and it's not particularly clear who initiated what, but you know that you're speaking and listening and being heard. Tango is a conversation, not just the conventional you talk-I listen type of conversation; tango can be the type of conversation in which neither of you really have to say anything, but you somehow understand each other, where you are so comfortable with each other that you can even live the silences together.[27] That is the kind of conversation tango can be.

[27] Inspired by a conversation with Collin Christopher, May 13, 2011.

Listen, Wait; Patience is a Virtue

Listening means being patient enough to wait and hear what someone has to say. It means that even if you think you already know what they're going to tell you, you wait anyway, just to make sure. Because having a conversation in which each time you try to say something the person you are speaking with assumes that she knows what you'll say and interrupts you, is pretty frustrating. It's not really a conversation if you don't get to talk, nor is it a conversation if you don't listen. So, listen, wait; patience is a virtue.

If you speak a lot in tango but forget to listen or anticipate and assume things that your partner hasn't said, it'll be more difficult to cultivate the sensitivity it takes to understand your partner's invitations and perceive the subtle nuances in the way he articulates his ideas; it will be more difficult to understand what your partner is asking of you or what your partner needs from you. Worse yet, you run the risk of fossilizing your dance by developing "defaults" – doing the same combinations over and over like a robot, impeding your own ability to take advantage of unexpected opportunities to spontaneously create new moves together. It's like when you get so engrained in a route that you start living in automatic, not paying attention. You take the same right at the same light that you take every other day and then you somehow find yourself pulling into your driveway.

And there's really no reason to rush each other. Be patient. It's not a race to get to the end of the sentence – each word counts. There's nothing wrong with pausing, regrouping, shifting weight a few times to see where she is and making sure you're on the same page. It's a constant game of adjusting to the person you are embracing, and that takes a fine-tuned ear.

As we develop a more consistent, more fluid connection, we can even interject things mid-sentence or add in tangents without disrupting the flow of the conversation, but enhancing it. If our intention is to hurry to finish each sentence and check it off our list, we'll miss these opportunities to add texture and character and to live our conversations.

Women are from Venus

What women want is a mystery that many men wish they could solve. It's true that at times we just seem to speak different languages. But when it comes down to it, we all simply want to be happy.

In tango, we speak with our body, and that's a language we can all understand. If you listen real carefully, you'll notice that she's showing you what she likes and asking for what she needs from you. If you listen to her body as it speaks to you, you'll know exactly what she wants.

Don't be too stubborn about the jumbled words you throw at each other. Sometimes words fall short, and we have to resort to hugs.

High Heels and Yellow Hippopotamuses

"Women are not babies," says Marcelo "El Chino" Gutierrez

Nor dolls, I'd say, for that matter.

"They are grown individuals and can make decisions for themselves," he says, "They do not need your help, just your respect."

Imagine if you wanted to go on a date and just grabbed her hand and dragged her to the restaurant. Chances are that when you let go, she'd be making the quickest exit possible. Invite her to come, and let her choose to walk with you. There's no need to "help" her.

One of the big problems is that leaders are often taught that "everything is the leader's fault." That's not true – it's a partnership. This mindset negates the responsibility and the presence of the follow. It also places too much pressure on leads to *make* things happen. Just like in a relationship, this can create problems of excessive tension and force. It's unfair and counterproductive for one person to be held solely responsible for communication, sex, musicality, etc.

Yes, since as a lead you are generally dealing with navigation issues and because the follow entrusts herself in your arms, it's a good idea to make sure that she does not get hurt and to avoid running her into tables. Taking care of her stops there. She does not need you to do the moves *for* her nor to physically carry her around the dance floor (sounds silly, but I have been carried around the dance floor once or twice).

Sometimes we want to help so much that we end up doing other people's tasks for them. We have four legs in tango, but they only move together as one creature if both people collaborate in making that happen. Try your best to be clear about what you are asking of her, and trust that she will try her best to understand you and meet you halfway. A partnership takes two.

Cars and women

I've heard men compare women in tango to cars. Some drive smooth and easy, like a Ferrari, while others are more like an old Volkswagen Bus and you've got to put in a little more elbow grease to get them to move. As much as I love this analogy, it makes an important point: not all women handle the same. So, fellas, take a little time to figure out how the car handles. Warm up the engine, start slowly and test-drive her. And if you find yourself with a Maserati in your arms or even a smooth BMW, please, please, don't jerk the gears around and stomp on the pedals like you might my old 1983 Toyota Tercel station wagon with the blue racing stripe – it's just not necessary and it might harm the vehicle.

* Note to drivers *

Please don't be mistaken: Your squeezing is not what makes me stay

Please don't be mistaken: your squeezing is not what makes me stay. No amount of squeezing will make me stay. I just want to embrace you and spend these tangos with you, so accept it and stop the squeezing. Please.

> *"El tango es una caricia a la mujer,"* told me El Chino Perico – "Tango is a caress for the woman." It's about embracing and making each other feel good.

Tango shouldn't require force. If you "need" to use force…

1) you are trying to do something your partner doesn't understand, so she doesn't know what to do. It's up to you to be more clear with your own body. She's listening to you, you have a captive audience – why would you yell?

2) your posture or relationship with your partner is actually blocking her movement and using force usually makes this worse. When you stop trying to make her do things, the focus shifts from what your partner isn't giving to what you can bring to the situation.

3) you might be trying to "protect" her; protecting her shouldn't hurt.

4) you are dancing for yourself; dance for her. Your timing might be different than her timing. Meet her where she's at instead of trying to force her into your idea of where she should be.

Just as you can't put a square peg in a round hole – as my friend Pete says, anything in life that requires too much force indicates that there is something wrong, period.

Calibrate

Calibrate the pair. Warm up the car a little bit. Check the fluids, the gears, tires – make sure all the parts are aligned. Check the machine before you pull out of the garage and definitely before you get on the highway or take her for a high-speed race!

Each person you dance with takes some adjustment. Like tuning an instrument, you tune to harmonize with each other. Sometimes it just feels right from the very beginning; sometimes there's an instant connection. But most often we need to take a little time to get to know each other. There are certain courting rituals, and they're there for a reason.

Slow down, take it easy. Patience pays off. Feel where your partner is, get comfortable with each other. This goes for both sides of the embrace. Gentlemen, make her feel safe in your arms and you'll be surprised what you can get away with (on the dance floor)! And ladies, be patient with him and with yourself. Don't just let your inner tigress pounce on him right away – you might scare him. Take your time to get accustomed to his lead before you pull out your latest dazzling embellishments. Be conscientious of each other and establish a connection and you'll be able to accomplish much more together than dancing tango by yourselves.

El tango es como el sexo

Cuando es bueno,
 te llega al alma,
 lo sentís en todo tu ser.

Pero cuando es malo,
 cuando es torpe,
 y no sentís una conexión,
 casi no lo podés aguantar
 y lo único que querés
 es que se acabe el momento.

Tango is like sex

When it's good,
 you get a rush,
 a feeling deep inside your core;
 it touches your soul, your essence.

But when it's bad,
 when it's awkward and clumsy,
 and you don't feel a connection,
 it's nearly unbearable
 and you can't wait for it to end.

Take it easy, start slow; develop the connection. "Plug in" to your partner. Once you have that and as long as you maintain it, there are no limits. Do whatever you want, but take your partner with you – do it *with* your partner. The difference is unbearably clear.

The Yellow Hippopotamus: A Woman's Presence

A man told me that with some women he can feel their presence, while with others it almost feels like they are not even there. It's something I think women often struggle with in tango, and in life. We are fed so many contradictory ideas about how a lady should be: light and elegant, strong yet delicate, confident yet modest. There are so many guidelines about how a lady should conduct herself, about her physical, emotional, and intellectual presence, that it's easy to get lost. We end up balancing on a tightrope, trying to be present, yet light as a feather.

With all these social complexes, it should be no surprise that when asked to lean against a man in public and walk around a dance floor, the inclination of many women is to try to make themselves as light and unobtrusive as possible. It is no wonder that many women end up feeling like a big yellow hippopotamus. Everyone is watching me and I'm so big and bulky and noticeable (no matter how thin they are). But who says a yellow hippopotamus can't be gracious and elegant? And if a yellow hippopotamus can carry herself in a way that is sexy and subtle, present and confident, so can all of us women!

The *tanguera*[28] is a real woman. She might be wide or short or slim or curvaceous, have hips, big feet, thighs. It's about learning to love yourself, learning to love even the things you don't like about yourself, carrying yourself with confidence.[29] If you can meet yourself where you're at, you can transform what you see as defects into virtues.[30] It's all about how you see yourself.

---

[28] *tanguera* – a woman who dances tango
[29] Rodolfo Dinzel, 2010.
[30] Inspired by a message from Karina Louro, May 2011.

Don't be afraid to wrap your arms around your partner and share yourself with him. Embrace him so that he feels your presence, and carry yourself with poise. You are a real woman, even if you feel like a yellow hippopotamus.

modern woman

In tango, the woman doesn't have to do everything alone. And it's more than ok; it's expected.

There's a lot of pressure on both men and women to be independent individuals. The pull toward individuality is so strong that it can be difficult for us to know how to act when we find a situation in which we don't have to stand alone. For the force drawing us inward, we push outward. When the feeling gets too intense, we step away.

Strong and independent I am, and proud of it. But do I build myself this strong fortress to protect myself from the risks of trusting? If we interact with our environment with rubber gloves and safety goggles, are we really experiencing it? Is it worth it to protect ourselves from pain at the expense of feeling?

When we embrace each other to dance, we have to choose to be present. Maybe it's that element of choice that makes it both so challenging and empowering at the same time. Choosing not to do everything alone is not a sign of weakness. Learning to collaborate doesn't imply diminishing yourself, it doesn't make you less independent, and it doesn't make you less of a woman. Let him open the pickle jar, make room for him in your life, trust, leap, because without trying, you'll be independent and alone. You don't have to lose yourself in order to connect with another person. Coalescing with another doesn't make you less – together, you can be more.

The higher the heel…

Ladies, if you dance tango, you know that men and the embrace are lovely and all, but beyond that, the true attraction to tango for many of us fashion-driven women is the tango high-heeled shoe. There are so many dizzying varieties of colors and prints and styles: with a flower, without the flower, tiger print, giraffe, 9cm, 10cm stiletto heels of anything from sexy black to flashy gold, yellow, red – you name it. Women come to Buenos Aires and go from one shoe store to another in search of that perfect pair… or two, or three, or more!

But, really, in a dance in which you spend so much time standing on one foot at a time, compromising your axis by sharing it with another in very close proximity to his toes (and yours aren't so far away either), why would anyone in their right mind complicate this already daring feat by slipping their feet into 3-inch heels, thus elevating their center of gravity that much further from the beloved Earth we all seek safety and solace from while praying not to fall over?

There actually are logical reasons to climb atop a high-heeled shoe in order to gracefully balance and walk, two as one.

In tango, we often need to have our weight in the metatarsal (the ball of the foot) and toes, like a feline, ready to pounce or react quickly to every one of our partner's indications. This is especially important when pivoting, because if your heel is on the floor, you are no longer pivoting around a single point. You actually don't have to lift your heel much[31] – just enough to be able to pivot. It's not about how high the heel is, it's how you work the floor. This is why people can dance tango in flat shoes or in 3-inch heels and barely lift their heels off the ground. And this is why I can float in my magic beige boots (that I like to wear with black, Horacio) and feel like I'm flying in my 7.5 cm heels.

Beyond the fashion, it's really about comfort. Depending on how high off the ground you like to raise the heel of your foot, having it already elevated can make it less work to take off. The high heel can keep you from having to do all the gymnastics of lifting your heel from the ground each time you need to do so. If you like to raise your heel a lot when you pivot, the high heel also helps maintain a consistent horizontal relationship to the floor that might be a little choppier without it because of all the up and down motion. And if you like to raise your heel quite a bit and try to avoid the long trip down to the ground, it's a lot of work for your legs.

Yes, you must be ready to react quickly, but that does not mean that you can never place your heel on the ground. You can use the high heel to rest and to receive weight when stepping. You can use it to connect with the floor more. You can also use it when playing with the quality you give your feet as they contact the floor or in your embellishments; you can play with your heel. You can even use it to stab the people next to you while doing the highest *boleos*[32] you can possibly muster, but I wouldn't recommend that. The high heel is a useful tool, a fashion

---

[31] You don't have to lift your heel much, especially if your heel raises as a consequence of your weight being in your metatarsals and your pushing the floor.

[32] *boleo* – a move where your free leg swivels around you or swings straight out and returns, either along the floor or in the air

accessory, and a social responsibility (and fellas, if it's on one of your four legs, it's partly your responsibility, too).

Is it necessary to dance tango with high heels on? No. One can dance tango without a high heel, but although it might sound silly without the above explanation, the high heels in tango (and the heights range as much as the people using them) serve a purpose....and it's not just because they're pretty.

The Rose is Just a Reminder

I'm dancing with you right now…

Contained by your embrace,
our bodies intertwined,
stepping together
through space and time,
I glance over your shoulder
and catch a glimpse
of the next potential dance,
of one whose arms I'd love to have around me,
and I begin to wonder how the timing
between our dances
and the next tango
will line up,
when he could possibly
ask me to dance with *him*…

And even though
I am encircled by your arms
and holding you in mine,
in my mind
I float farther and farther away.

But what if that next potential dance
never comes to be?
What if the timing won't be quite right?
If he'll have already asked somebody else?

If we cross paths stepping
across the threshold
of the room with the wooden dance floor?
If he has somewhere else to go?
If someone else who I overlooked
ends up asking me to dance?

And while all this is passing through my mind,
what if the feeling
of your body pressed against mine,
your arms around me,
your breathing and your movements
– your essence
escapes me?
Or worse: I never truly embrace it;
I mean, what if I never truly embrace you?

What if while I'm occupied with thoughts
of what will happen,
or what won't happen,
or what was,
I fail to grasp the beauty of what is,
the gift you are offering me
during these three minutes of our lives
that we will never be able to repeat,
that we'll never get back again?

What if between the anguish of what could be
and the scrutiny of what was,
I miss what *is*?
What if between my thoughts of
the future that might never be
and the past that can no longer be changed,
I miss living the present?

What if instead of dancing with you,
feeling your movements,
reading your body,
and seeing into your soul,
I spend my energy
on something that doesn't even exist?

The last tango has already passed.
The next tango has yet to be.
But right now,
at this moment,
I readjust my arm laid across your back
and breathe in your existence.
I fill the spaces you provide
as invitations
to participate in our dialogue
with my thoughts,
my ideas,
my emotions,
my presence.

At this moment,
right now,
until the *chun chun* marks the end of the tango,
until we release our arms from around one another,
I am dancing with you.

In the Moment

"Between the regrets of your past and your anxieties about the future, is you," says Rodolfo Dinzel. Trying to relive the past or getting caught up in my future plans, I catch myself missing out on my present. Between what was and will be, there is; I am.

It's easy to get entangled in our past. Once we get a taste of something good, we can spend our lives searching for it again. After an amazing dance during which my friend and I danced an entire tango in one little square, just playing, I wanted another. The next time I saw him I was eager to recreate that tango, but it was totally different. At some point I realized that my frustration with not finding that amazing dance from a few days before got in the way of my enjoying the dance we were actually dancing. Appreciate what is, *porque esperando lo que no es, te perdés lo que es* – because waiting for what isn't, you miss what is.

And as far as the future goes, sometimes our plans work out differently than we anticipated, and that's ok. In 2010, I decided that I would live in Buenos Aires for a year. A few months into it, I realized that it no longer made the best sense for me. Why tie myself to my plans? Why limit myself by the vision I had yesterday when I see things differently today? Why create a box for myself? Doesn't it make sense to adjust as you go?

If we are made up mostly of water and our planet is mostly water, why have we created and continue to perpetuate rigidity in our society and our lives? Flow and let flow. *Se hace lo que se puede con lo que hay* – do what you can with what you have. Anything too rigid in life is worth reexamining. Living the present – that part between our past and our future – is so liberating, because instead of stressing about the reality you wish you had, you're working with the reality you actually have.

The past is important. It informs our present – that felt good, can we do that again, please? But it isn't our present. Having hope for the future keeps us going, but the beauty of life is in every moment that we breathe, every chance we have to smile, every excuse we find to let out an uninhibited, unapologetic laugh. Dream big, stretch your imagination, but in the hope of reaching the moon, don't miss the flowers that blossom at your feet.[33]

Living in the moment means asking yourself, what are the possibilities now? And now? And now? It means constantly reevaluating and adjusting, rather than stubbornly sticking with a plan that no longer makes sense. The beauty is that you get to invent and reinvent yourself as you go. By doing this, you get more in tune with your partner, with the people around you, with your present, and with yourself.

Between the past and the future, is the present, the moment; live in the moment, dance in the moment.

---

[33] "In the hope of reaching the moon men fail to see the flowers that blossom at their feet." – Albert Schweitzer

Dos guitarras y un abrazo desconocido… en el Subte!
Two guitars and the embrace of a stranger… in the Subte!

As I watch the metal stairs get swallowed up below me and descend into the still air of the *subte* (subway), the melody of a tango on the strings of two guitars moves through me. I scramble in search of *monedas* (change) to give the two musicians. Dropping the change in one of their open cases, I answer their thank-you nod with, *"Tengo muchas ganas de bailar. ¡Gracias!"* – I really want to dance. Thank you! And as my feet touch the platform, they can no longer contain themselves; they begin caressing it, drawing circles and making lines.

"¿Estás practicando?" asks a man's voice, are you practicing?

"¿Bailás?" Do you dance?

"Sí."

Before the word leaves his lips, my left arm is reaching around his back and my right extends to find his left.

"¿Bailamos un tanguito?" but it's not really a question, as we begin a silent conversation of two bodies walking as one, two guitars, one tango. The song ends and the lights of the Subte B train approach, doors open, and the irreproducible moment has passed.

My Facebook status that day:

> *¡Que suerte encontrar una persona justo en el momento que lo necesitás que te puede dar precisamente lo que precisás! ¡Y el hombre baila!*

> What amazing luck to encounter a stranger who is just the right person at precisely the right time! And the man could dance!

Touch-the-Core-of-Your-Being Healing

I walk around as if in a dream, pensive without thinking about anything in particular. My thoughts are fuzzy as are my strides. I don't feel the weight of my footsteps against the stone slabs of the sidewalks; I don't have a particular destination. A serene quiet envelops me as I cross streets, look in windows, admire the flowers around me. This is the quiet after the storm.[34] I am all alone with my thoughts and my body walks without much calculation.

I move in slow motion and somehow my feet take me to the familiar wooden door, down the long corridor, to the patio where I go through the motions of greeting the people in what has become my safe place.[35] With particularly low energy this day, I make my way over to the bar on the far wall and begin my stretching, my little Zen, connect-with-myself and meditate routine. The room whirls with dancers around me, on a different frequency.

A tap on my shoulder. It's Miguel. Sometimes he just knows. And somehow I feel the shell of myself wrap my arms around him as his arms contain me and his energy fills the holes of what is missing in me. Like this, with his presence, I am able to give him four or five good tangos. I put all of myself into those tangos and by the last one, I have nothing left to give. I feel empty, a relieving kind of empty, an empty ready to be filled with goodness, like after making love and releasing everything, deeply and profoundly, touch-the-core-of-your-being emotional.

I sit on the tile floor of the patio, lean against the wall, close my eyes and exhale.

---

[34] We lost Grandpa Carl in August and Grandma Caty in October 2009.
[35] The Dinzel Studio

If…

November 2, 2009

A friend asked how I'm doing and if I saw this guy I had mentioned to her, and what I was about to write in response was: "Wish I was hanging out with the guy, but…" BUT I've been trying to tell myself to live in the moment, I remembered, and enjoy the present and stop worrying about how much better things might be IF… if I had a dreamy lover, if I found a great dance partner who wanted to train more intensely, if it was warmer outside, if… IF!

> What I should be saying is that I have been good, real good. Yesterday afternoon I finally made it to Chinatown here in Buenos Aires, where I found *hum bao* rolls and seafood – seafood that's supposed to be the best in the city and not that expensive. At night I went to a *milonga* with Linda. It was an eventful night because it was the club owner's birthday and there were performances (including Alberto Podestá singing) and cake and, of course, dancing. I wore the ¾ length fishnet stockings my cousin Maria gave me when I was leaving Chişinău, and I could've sworn this old guy with a large belly was yelling at the guy I was dancing with to turn me again so my skirt would go up! And today I went to the store with the dance tennis shoes and bought a pair and my feet are oh, so happy!

So I have to say that I'm doing alright and trying to appreciate the little things in life and live in the present. Now, if I only…

There's always time to smell the roses

As I caught myself walking past a rose one day and wondering what it smelled like, I had an internal conversation to justify my uninterrupted trajectory. But I had already passed it and I had to keep moving forward. But it would look silly to turn around and walk back to smell it, I reasoned with myself.

And it was then, hearing myself rationalize why I couldn't smell the rose, that I decided that when I pass a rose and that little voice inside me wonders if it smells nice, I'll stop to smell it. I made an agreement with myself to smell the roses, because there's never time to smell the roses, if you don't make time.

Smelling the rose is about more than just the act of taking in its lovely fragrance and if I miscalculate the distance, it's petals tickling my nose – it's about pausing, taking a moment out of my busy running around to connect with another part of myself.

The rose is just a reminder.

Dance like Water

"Mistakes" are just unanticipated opportunities

When I confessed to a friend that I need to stop making the wrong choices in love, I expected her to answer something along the lines of, yes, grow up. But instead she replied, not every relationship has to be a lifelong union and if such is not the case, it doesn't mean it was a poor decision. Some things are meant to last for longer periods of time than others. Just because something doesn't last the happily-ever-after it supposedly should, doesn't mean that it wasn't what I needed at the time.

There are no wrong choices. We make choices based on what we feel or need. It's unfair to judge our decisions later on as wrong because we obviously chose them for a specific reason which at that particular moment and in that context made sense. We're used to right and wrong, black and white, but life isn't always so simple. All we can give is the best we've got and that's the most anyone can really ask of us. Tango is an imperfect union between two perfectly imperfect people.

The concept of "mistakes" implies that there is a way things should be that is different from the way they are. If you shift your focus from what "should be" to what is, you can meet each dance partner where they're at. Then you can start connecting with the person you are dancing with, instead of being anxious about the ideal you were taught. You can start connecting with yourself and figuring out what works for you and building on that, rather than fixating on what doesn't. There are no mistakes – only opportunities to explore movements other than what you had intended, to adapt to your partner and listen to each other and create together. And that's what it's all about.

Improvisation

Improvising is doing something for which you have no predetermined outcome or script. We know that we'll embrace each other and that we'll make our way around the dance floor, but we have no idea exactly what will happen during each tango. That's the beauty of it.

During one of his chats about theory, Rodolfo Dinzel was talking about how tango is improvised and the fact that the pair creating the figures and shapes can never truly observe themselves and that each moment is fleeting and can't be recreated. Someone asked him to repeat a phrase. At a loss for the exact word combination he had just uttered, he smiled and said, "Sorry, my words, my dialogue, are improvised – I can't repeat them."

We know how to improvise, Rodolfo says, we do it all the time in our daily lives. We interact with and react to our surroundings. Conversations are all acts of improvisation. We don't know exactly what we'll say or how someone will respond and how we will continue the exchange after that. We do, however, have some logical parameters that govern our conversations: we know which words are appropriate to a specific situation, that when getting on the bus it doesn't make sense to say "the bread is stale," that the choice of tense alters the meaning of a sentence, that some sounds, although I am capable of producing them, will not make sense if they are not part of the commonly-accepted realm of sounds for that particular language.[36] But improvise, we do.

---

[36] Seminar on Improvisation in Tango, Rodolfo Dinzel, 2010.

Improvising means being flexible

"Like water in a stream making its way down the plain," says Rodolfo Dinzel. "Water is not stubborn: if it comes to an obstacle in its way, it flows around it. Dance like water."

...like "Sea-weed":

> Sea-weed sways and sways and swirls
> As if swaying were its form of stillness;
> And if it flushes against fierce rock
> It slips over it as shadows do, without hurting itself.
>
> – D.H. Lawrence[37]

It means that even though you might have spent your day dreaming about the chocolate gateau cake and the kitchen sent out the last portion just before you got to the restaurant, you can still enjoy your evening.

It means that even though you planned a series of three *sacadas*[38] but you and your partner didn't quite get there for the third one, it's ok.

It means that we keep going, even when things don't go how we expect, even when the road gets rough:

Like my friend who told me about his store getting robbed. That's awful! Yes, but sometimes things are just so good that you need a little something to wake you up, he said.

---

[37] sent to me by Greg Constantino after a conversation about "flowing like water"

[38] *sacada* – a move that gives the illusion of kicking your partner's leg or foot out of the way

Or when I can't find something and in the process of looking for it, I get reacquainted with all the other things I have and maybe reorganize or downsize – before finding my sunglasses on my head.

It means that in the absence of a schedule, I start waiting for the bus when I reach the bus stop.

It means that in order to enjoy the light of a candle, you have to let it burn and melt away.

It means that even those moments in our lives that we wish we could hold on to, that we hope will never end, do end. Change is constant; nothing stays the same. Sometimes we focus so much on wanting the feeling to last, that we miss the true beauty of the moment itself.

Life is a game of improvisation.

It's the obstacles in our way, big or small, the tough decisions, the forks in the road – our interactions with the changing people around us who act not always as we'd expect – that cause us to shift and create and live. Sway like seaweed. Don't fight the rocks in your path, flow around them; dance like water.

Good things happen in small spaces

Lo bueno siempre viene en frasco chico – good things come in small packages, says my friend Karina. If you have less of something, it becomes more precious; you're more careful about how you use it. When everything is handed to us and it's easy, we don't have to work for it and we don't have to be as creative. Ingenuity comes from necessity. That's why our Bunica Caty[39] was able to amaze my brother, my cousin, and me with stuffed animals she made out of scraps of things she found around her house in Moldova and why I was so proud of the table I built from shelves I found in a plaza. We make things happen, even when it seems impossible. Our problems in life don't come with solutions; that's what makes them problems, and it's up to us to solve them.

In Seattle (my home base), we are used to having lots of space. Everything is big: our streets, our supermarkets, our personal bubbles. It's no surprise that this would translate to our dance floors, too. *I need space to try out all the figures I've been learning,* you might reason. Yes, in a practice environment maybe that would be helpful, at first, but tango is about improvising and adapting and interacting with those around you. Lack of space can actually provide you with more stimulation to invent new moves, moves that are so cool that you might never have come up with them if it weren't for the couple in front of you taking an unexpected step back and those on the left squeezing you toward the edge of the dance floor. Those are the moments that cause you to change your game plan and think on your toes, or even better, to feel.

---

[39] *bunică* – Romanian for "grandma"

Tango is all about figuring out how to work with small spaces, how to make something amazing out of something as simple as an embrace. It's about dancing close to your partner, comments a man in the film *Tango Baile Nuestro*: *"El tango nació para bailarse tomado porque el verdadero tango es para la pareja. Tiene que bailar no suelto porque usted tiene una justeza, hay poco lugar para poner los pies. Si yo bailo a 50 cm de la mujer, yo puedo hacer cualquier cosa, como bailar boogie o el rock* – Tango was born to be danced very close because real tango is for the couple to dance. You need accuracy; there is little room to put your feet. If I dance 50 cm from the woman I can do anything, like dance boogie or rock."[40] In tango, you can do more with less. It's about finding new ways to wrap your bodies around each other so that the space you need in order to move, you create within your embrace – without pushing away from each other but by getting closer to one another.

We spend so much energy stressing and even obsessing over what we don't have. It's amazing how much changes when we shift our focus from anxiety over the space we wish we had to appreciation of and creativity with the precious little space we *do* have.

---

[40] Jorge Zanada, dir., *Tango Baile Nuestro,* Film. 1988.

Sight-dependency

During a training session on visual impairment and blindness for The Northwest School's Summer Program, I was introduced to the idea of "sight-dependency": those of us who are accustomed to using our sight in our daily lives are dependent on it. People that have less sight or no sight are less dependent on this sense and use other senses to help them perceive their surroundings.[41] In a dance that has to do with speaking and sensing with your body, many of us are far too sight-dependent. Yes, sight is useful when navigating the dance floor, but I have danced with my eyes closed with a man who is blind. And I've seen people without sight dance together and make it around a dance floor just fine.

You have to see it to believe it – but there are things you can't see, and it can be more difficult to perceive them if you're busy trying to see them. Since the fancy things in tango happen down below, it can be tempting to try to see what's going on. But if you look down enough to see exactly where your feet are or where your partner's feet are, chances are your posture is complicating your relationship with your partner.

Imagine a relationship in which you didn't trust yourself enough to be confident about where you stand or were constantly second-guessing your partner. If you rely on your crutch – your sense of sight, it's less likely that you'll develop the ability to perceive your partner's presence by feeling his body. In order to get to know each

---

[41] Training at the Northwest School by Yang-su Cho and Mark Adreon, Seattle, June 2010: It's as if people who can see have a handicap because they rely on their sense of sight, whereas people who cannot see find a way to function without this sense.

other, you have to find a way to let go of or move past some of these insecurities and trust.

Resist the temptation to look at her feet to figure out where she is. If you aren't sure, just ask, with your body. Luckily, we have two legs so there are only two options here. It's a gamble of 50-50. There are many ways to ask without resorting to looking down: shift weight once or twice, walk on the outside so that you don't run the risk of stepping on her, or invite her to move around you while you stay in place.

Dance with your eyes closed – even leads! – or at least, dance as if your sight is just for navigation purposes.[42] Try to visualize where he stands, where his legs are, where his feet come in contact with the floor, think a real-time, computer-generated scan of the volume of his body (with green lines like in *The Matrix*). Feel where his weight is from the contact in your embrace. The idea is that you communicate to your partner where you are and he communicates to you where he is. The more you trust that you can understand your partner, the less you have to double-check with your eyes. Trust the signals she gives you and you will become more and more aware of where she is and what space you have to work with.

We can't analyze and calculate everything; sometimes we just have to let go and feel. It's real-time, live, now. Cultivate the ability to sense where the space is and isn't, trust all of your senses, and you'll no longer be so sight-dependent. And remember that you can hug and play all at the same time.

---

[42] On a tightly-packed dance floor, sometimes you can even *sense* where the couples around you are – I call this "The Seaweed Effect."

Language and Grammar

Verbal languages are a natural result of the need to communicate with one another. We change and adapt them as we need. We add in words that seem to be lacking, join words together for fun or practical purposes, and change words to make them easier to say. Words that go out of fashion or no longer make sense, we use less and less. And as we speak, we improvise, searching for the best way to express our thoughts. Languages are dynamic.

In order to explain languages, some people observe and record patterns which they call grammar. They write books and books full of grammar and exercises to practice this grammar. But language does not exist because of grammar; language exists because of the need to express ideas and share them with others. Grammar exists because of language, not the other way around. This is why dictionaries and grammar books struggle to keep up with the constant changes in spoken language.

If you spend all your time memorizing exercises from a book, you end up speaking like a textbook – stiff, rigid. If you learn the essence of the words, you can play with how you string them together and make choices that reflect what you want to express, that reflect your personality. It's like the difference between learning to follow a recipe and learning to play with food (cook).

If what we aspire to achieve when learning a verbal language is fluency, why would we not apply the same concepts to a physical language, like tango? Sequences can be useful for learning techniques, but don't let your study of grammar hamper your ability to communicate, to comprehend and express yourself. Olga Besio says, *"El tango es un baile popular, improvisado... hay que hacer que las figuras salgan solas* – tango is an improvised, popular dance… you have to make the figures come out on their own [naturally].”

Language is always changing. Seek the essence of the words so that you can put together your own sentences and build a real, live dialogue. As you search for different ways to relate to your partner, you’ll develop the ability to adapt to each other’s bodies and create a fluid conversation composed of moves that take shape as you speak.

We don't have the same "vocabulary"...

Regarding the lack of a structured system for teaching tango across the board (tango deliberations over a glass of wine, or two):

"Everyone learns different skills," complained a friend, "so we don't have a common vocabulary."

My reply: "That means you each have more to offer one another in the conversation."

You don't need to know certain prerequisites before you can step out onto the dance floor. Tango starts as soon as you make eye contact and your gazes intertwine – embraced, you are dancing tango. Tango is about the discovery of something new in each step, in each embrace, each time you dance. The beauty is that you will hopefully never know all of the same "vocabulary" or the same ways to apply this vocabulary; that you will continue to find nuances and qualities and movements and things that surprise you. In the common language that is the embrace you build together, you can say anything.

Paint Outside the Lines

No puedes hacer adornos en el tiempo fuerte – The Strong Beat

"No puedes hacer adornos en el tiempo fuerte – you can't do adornments on the strong beat," said a teacher.

Why? I asked myself. And after class, I asked him to elaborate. I wanted to make sure that I understood the idea I disagreed with:

"Porque generalmente el hombre te va a marcar un paso en el tiempo fuerte," he explained – "because generally, the man will lead a step on the strong beat"... and I [as the follow] might not make it.

Wait a minute. Brakes!!! Make it to what? Make it how? What the hell does the strong beat have to do with anything? If I'm attentive to my partner and I feel that there's time to add in an adornment, I do it, or I make time by asking him to wait for me. On the strong beat, the half beat, the melody, with the bandoneón, the piano, the guitar, during a pause, because I'm adding something to the musical conversation, whenever I feel inspired to do so. If the guy leads something that doesn't give me time to do an adornment on the half beat, when I supposedly *can* do an adornment, can I do the adornment anyway? Obviously, the objective is to express myself while dancing *with* my partner. If I can play and stay with him or invite him to come with me, that's what counts.

I think this logic or this way of looking at musicality doesn't make sense alongside the idea that the follow needs to be sensitive to what the lead is asking of her, at any point in the music, not to mention that the lead needs to pay attention to where the follow's at, too. Leave room for feeling your partner and being responsive to the human you are interacting with – *¡no bailes en automático!* – don't dance in automatic! And if you're always leading a step on the strong beat, how about you switch it up a bit and try other ways of interacting with the music? Musicality is not just about when you step and definitely extends beyond the strong beat.

Horacio Godoy, known for his manner of playing with music in his dance, responded to the above scenario (my conversation with the other teacher) by saying: "*Es un baile popular; no hay síes y no hay noes* – It's a popular dance; there are no yes's and there are no no's… even a 'mistake'," he said, "you can do something with." And in the class immediately after, he demonstrated other ways of interacting with the strong beat – an adornment the woman can add or an extra circle the man can lead to accentuate the strong beat. The danger of counting the strong beat, Horacio said, *"es que nos quedamos con el tiempo fuerte* – is that we can get stuck with the strong beat," when there's so much more to play with.

I spent some time talking about this with other people, too, and my friend Tim Savatieff stated it nicely: "Careful with absolute statements," he said, "like always and never."

Pintar sin Límites – Paint Outside the Lines

¿Qué es lo malo de pintar sin límites,
sin saber el tamaño del cuadro,
sin saber que herramientas vas a necesitar,
de irse sin planes,
de pintar fuera de las líneas?
Creatividad nace del no saber,
inteligencia de la necesidad.
¿Qué es lo malo de perderse
si es para encontrarse otra vez?

What's so bad about painting without limits,
without knowing the size of the picture,
without knowing what tools you'll need?
What's so bad about leaving without a plan,
about painting outside the lines?
Intelligence is born of the unknown;
creativity arises from necessity.
What is so bad about getting lost
so that you can find yourself again?

Lines and Limits

I think that sometimes we get so used to seeing the lines that we forget why they're there. We get confused. We forget that someone made lines to create boundaries to simplify things. That the lines weren't always there, that things can exist, that we can exist without them; that the lines exist because we continue to see them, because we perpetuate them. We continue to view the world through them. We are, not because of the lines; we existed before and continue despite them. They're there because somebody put them there.

Limits that Limit vs. Limits that Inspire

Whereas limits are what push us to think outside the box, they can also teach us not to think for ourselves. It's the difference between building things from an instruction manual (where you are limited by the instructions) and just grabbing blocks out of a bucket to see what you can create (where you are limited by the number and shape of blocks in the bucket). People that have a talent in the realm might learn a lot from the instruction manual, but especially those who struggle, will learn to depend on it.

When communicating and connecting with your partner is the ultimate goal, limits that require you to work together to find solutions – such as restrictions in space – can be really beneficial. On the other hand, limits that diminish the focus on communication between you – predetermined sequences of steps, for example – can hinder your ability to connect with and adapt to each other. The danger of structure is that it can limit by giving the illusion of helping. Be careful not to get stuck repeating patterns and forget about your partner.

Structures applied to musicality are dangerous, too. Applying a pattern to a dance that is based on dancing what you feel is in no way different than telling people how and where to put their foot on step one, step two, step three. If interacting with and expressing what you hear in the music is the objective, telling someone that they're not "ready" to experiment with the melody at this "stage" of their learning or tying a particular move (a *sacada*, for example) or sequence to a specific part of the music, limits in a way that detaches the student from the process of learning to express what the music makes him feel.

Amplify the possibilities by drawing attention to different parts of the music; show people different ways that you express what you hear in the music and different places where a *sacada* might be useful; give them ideas. Because playing doesn't have to start once you reach a certain "level" – it's all a game of improvisation, of trying and exploring and searching. And the *sacada* can happen whenever you determine that it expresses what you hear and feel and flows well in your interaction with your partner.

Limits are powerful. There's a difference between limits that push you to explore and limits that cause dependency – the difference is in how you apply the limit. Teach your students skills. Teach them to listen, to explore; teach them to push the limits and find new ways of seeing things. Stimulate creativity. Inspire them to challenge themselves to be better than they imagine they can be. And when you employ limits in your teaching, determine whether they help or hinder your students.

Give a child a blank piece of paper and a box of crayons and let him explore, let him think, let him feel. Let him find his own limits by pushing the envelope and then pushing some more. Let him fall, so he can figure out a way to keep going; so he can pick himself up and learn that falling's not so scary.

Aprender el Camino – Find your way

Con un mapa, aprendés a leer el mapa.
Sin mapa, aprendés a buscar el camino;
Aprendés a caminar.

With a map, you learn to read the map.
Without a map, you learn to find your way;
You learn to walk on your own.

Cooking is playing with food

Rather than following a recipe verbatim, experiment with the ingredients to see what each one adds. Try different proportions and combinations. Scoop a little taste of the sauce onto your tongue and experience it. Tantalize your taste buds. If you can figure out what makes the recipe work and understand how different ingredients get along with one another, you can play with it – you can improvise.

The only rule is the embrace

Tango started as a game of improvisation, explains Rodolfo Dinzel: there were no figures and sequences, no patterns to follow. The only rule was the embrace; that is what made tango different. People explored what they could do in relation to their partner while maintaining the connection. As time passed, those who were less skilled at this game of improvisation and spontaneity created patterns to help them understand and explain what they saw. Much of what is taught today is a written and systematized version of this improvised game.

But the essence of tango is not each specific figure; it is learning techniques for interacting with the body of your partner. You don't need patterns to follow. By developing an awareness of each other, you can co-create things you might never imagine, fleeting things that you can't put in your pocket or show your friends. Things that happen in the moment, due to those specific circumstances, to the space you both create in between the crevices of each other's bodies. Once we start to recreate and reproduce them systematically, they lose their authenticity and we get tangled in recreating a past that is no longer – we get detached from the moment and from each other. Then the task becomes to find each other again.

They don't listen to the music...

When I sat down to talk with El Chino Perico my last Saturday in Buenos Aires, I had some questions in mind. One was about musicality, because I had come across a camp that told me things like *"no hay que hacer adornos en el tiempo fuerte* – you can't do embellishments on the strong beat" and *"la sacada tiene que ser en un punto importante de la música* – the *sacada* has to coincide with an important part of the music." I wanted to know what this smooth-dancing, older gentlemen had to say about this.

His response: *"No escuchan la música* – they don't listen to the music," and to my dismay, I thought he belonged to that same group – it can't be! We kept talking and somehow we got back to music and he said, *"El bailarín es uno más de la orquesta* – the dancer is one more musician in the orchestra," something I had heard before at the Dinzel Studio. But how did his two statements fit together?

It wasn't until I was revising this book one day in Seattle and reflecting on my workshop on musicality, that I came to a realization. What I think El Chino Perico was saying about musicality was that people don't listen to the music, not that they don't dance like they're "supposed to" or follow some pattern, but exactly that: they dance patterns and don't actually listen to the music. That is really the only way that you can dance "outside" the music in tango, a free-form dance with no specific structure, a dance in which it's the manner of doing it not the form, the how not the what, that counts.

Dueño de mis silencios – Master of my silences

In tango you are free to say "yes" and free to say "no" – free to move and free to pause. "In tango, I am the master of my silences," says Rodolfo Dinzel.

The music doesn't dictate your steps. You play with it as if you were another instrument – "like a jam-session in jazz!" exclaimed Terry as we chatted one day. That's why you can look at a room full of people all dancing tango to the same music, but each couple is doing something different and each individual might be doing something different within the pair, too. Yet they are all dancing tango together.

It's not necessary to chase the music, to hit every single beat; it's not a Dance Dance Revolution[43] game where you have to step on each shape coming your way or you don't get all the points. Choose the beats you do movements for, find other ways to interact with the music. There are so many layers in the music, so many ways to play with it in all the dimensions of our bodies, in the way we relate to our partner, in the space we occupy on the dance floor. Please don't limit yourself to pre-packaged patterns and counting beats. Rather than "moving" yourself to the music, listen to the music, listen carefully. Pretend it's an old friend telling you a story and let his words move you – that honest impulse reaction that happens before you can even think to control it. And savor the pauses as well as the movements, because in tango, those count, too.

The only way to be "outside" the music is to not listen to the music and dance the same regardless of which tango you're dancing to. *"El tango,"* says a woman in a documentary

---

[43] An interactive dance game found in arcades and for home entertainment systems.

about tango in Villa Urquiza,[44] *"inspira... haces la figura que salió en este momento y capaz que la quieres hacer en otro tango y no va* – Tango inspires... you do a step that came about in that moment and maybe you want to do it in another tango and it just doesn't fit."

So, when you ask me how to interpret Piazzolla, I say, *"Como te canta el culo* – however the hell you want," because that's something no one can give you. It's that piece of yourself that you put into your dance that gives life to your movements, and like El Pibe Sarandí said, "Your elegance, your personality, your presence and the grace of your movements is in your soul. *Yo no te puedo dar mi alma* – I can't give you my soul."[45]

---

[44] Jorge Zanada, dir., *Tango Baile Nuestro,* Film. 1988.
[45] Ricardo Maceiras "El Pibe Sarandí," www.elpibesarandi.com.ar.

A Reciprocal Relationship

The Active "Follow"

If it's a "conversation," a "dialogue," it means it takes two people. In the documentary *La Confitería Ideal: The Tango Salon,* Javier Rodriguez says of Geraldine: "I lead everything…but I listen, I wait for her, sometimes I hurry her when she gets caught up on a tangent…we talk." "Not with words," clarifies Geraldine.[46]

Being an *active* "follow"[47] doesn't necessarily mean "doing things." Tango isn't just about "things" and "moves"; it has so many dimensions. Being active doesn't mean fighting with your partner either. Being an active follow means letting him know you're there. It means letting him know what you need. It means being an active part of the giving and taking process; being attentive, being present, being you. He's dancing with a person, not a broomstick. Each step you do, each time you move across space together, even the pauses, you choose to be there. It's about taking ownership of the part you play in making up the whole, knowing that you have a voice in the union you create together.

---

[46] Geraldine Rojas and Javier Rodriguez in *La Confitería Ideal: The Tango Salon,* BBC 4 Documentary, 2005.

[47] The term "active follow" sounds a bit contradictory, no? How are you a follower but active? Other terms used to describe the woman in tango include *la mujer* (the woman) or *la compañera* (the companion). The woman in tango is not just a "follower," she's an integral part of a partnership.

The Logistics

So, logistically speaking, how does one go from being a "passive follow" or simply a "follow," a receiver, to being a taker and a giver in this dance?

Coming from the Dinzel Studio where tango is a dance of 50-50, I've spent a lot of time and energy working on how to introduce this concept to people that might be of the mindset that the responsibility of the dance is the man's and that the roles are either "lead" or "follow." Whereas some leads are very adamant about their role as the one who calls the shots, many just haven't been taught to listen – it doesn't mean that they don't want to hear what you have to say. Keep in mind that your lead might be really receptive to the idea of a dialogue right away, or it might take a little time for him (and for you) to adjust. That's not the opposite of being receptive: this approach might be new to him. *Ablandálo* – soften him up, knead him gently, ease into it. It doesn't have to be all or nothing. Be patient with him, but don't give up on putting your personality into the dance. It takes practice, both for a follow who has been taught only to receive and for a lead who has been taught just to speak.

Just as leads take their time to feel out their follows, follows should do the same with their leads. There are many ways to explore being more active. Although sometimes a little shock to shake the status quo is necessary, in general, I'd suggest starting small and subtle. Make your walk denser to slow things down or speed up an *ocho*.[48] Make sure he's listening so you don't end up having a monologue. Wait for him just as you'd want him to wait for you. Ask him for the

---

[48] From my experience, slowing down is usually easier to start out with.

changes you want from the role of the follow – you don't have to reconfigure your arms to participate in the dance. Think of it like coaxing him into sharing a dessert with a smile, a gentle caress of his arm.

Starting small might not sound like a revolution. If you measure it in size, it might seem quite insignificant. But bigger is not always better and what you gain by taking it slowly with your partner and making sure he feels comfortable with the change is monumental. Not only is it helpful for your lead if you avoid startling him, but it's also great training for you. By starting with subtle changes, you develop the skill of perceiving and modifying the more intricate details. It takes practice. Over time, you'll discover different ways to contribute to the dance. Soon you'll be able to add onto moves he leads, changing the quality, the intensity, the speed, the size, the direction, etc.[49]

Eventually, you might find leads with whom you can even propose movements. Ok, so that means you have to start taking classes and paying attention to how to "lead" sequences, develop your vocabulary, right? You already know many moves because tango is a reciprocal process. You know how it feels to be led through a certain figure, you know what you need, so just ask your partner to make that space for you. Think about what you like – that if he does something to move one leg, your weight is on the other leg, that he waits to make sure you're coming along, that he speaks to you with his body. What's comfortable for you will most likely feel good to him, too. There's no need to memorize steps and sequences. It's an option, but you are already so good at listening that you can find those

---

[49] Rodolfo Dinzel often suggests that his students experiment with modifying the amplitude, velocity, angle, etc. of their movements.

moments where there's time or space to add something in or change the direction, or you can create them yourself by letting him know when you want to suggest something. Get his attention and when you know he's listening, invite him to come with you. Assess the correlation between your bodies as you go, feel the possibilities in each moment; improvise.

A common technical question is whether or not the follow then has to take responsibility for navigation. Yes and no. It depends on how you work together. Follows can open their eyes and help with navigation and make sure that if they propose a move or a change in direction, the space is clear and it does not cause the couple to collide with another couple or object. Or, even as an active follow, you can dance with your eyes closed as long as you are extra sensitive to your partner's navigational maneuvers. You can suggest and modify things in the dance, knowing that your partner will notify you if there is a greater need for the two of you to change directions to avoid a collision or move down the dance floor. If you are both sensitive to each other, you will understand who needs what, when and how.

Walking with Style

I'm not sure how I feel about the term "embellishment" or "adornment." Somehow it makes it sound like these details are superfluous to the dance (and those that really are superfluous could maybe be forgone). They're style, but so is all of tango. "Tango is walking with style," said Laura at the America del Sur Hostel the night I arrived in Buenos Aires. Both the follow and the lead add their own personal touch to the dance. It's the difference between just doing the steps and dancing. And where exactly do we separate the "embellishments" from the dance itself?

Mutual Respect

Chun! Chun! The tango ends as I whip my leg up to hook it around high up on his thigh.

"You know, some good dancers wouldn't like that in a milonga," Stefan Barth says, "unless they lead it."

"Really?" I'm a little surprised, since guys are "supposed to" like all intimate touching done unto them by a woman, or so society seems to say.

"Yes. It's about respecting boundaries," he goes on to explain. "Do you like it if a man touches you without your permission? The entire tango is about asking your permission to get close to you and women should do the same; they should respect a man's space and ask permission, see if he's accepting the advance before you follow through with it."

Tango is about sharing your partner's space. When women want to do something to their partner's body or use their partner's personal space, there is a way to communicate that and to make sure it's ok. "I am not here to be like that bar on the wall," he points to the ballet bar we use for exercises and stretching.

There are ways and there are ways.

A Place of 50-50

We can get to a place of 50-50,
where the connection feels so fluid
that it doesn't matter who leads what
but that we move together.
Where my body
and my partner's body are one.
Where, together,
we are one entity.

Where my legs are his
and his legs are mine
and we have one heartbeat between us,
and, if even for just three minutes,
we forget about everything else,
we let go of our inhibitions and our fear
of not knowing who's in charge,
we breathe together,
we feel each other,
we share our souls.

Follow the Leader!

Are you leading or am I? Who's the leader? Does it matter? We see things through the prism of power structures we are accustomed to, of hierarchies and upside down pyramids: someone is always in charge (the leader(s)) and someone else is always submissive, passive, choosing (albeit "autonomously") to follow. One listens, the other one talks. Pass the "talking stick."[50] If we come across structures that we are familiar with, everything is ok. You lead, I'll follow? I lead, so you follow.

But what happens when there is no one person who leads and no one person who follows – when both people lead and both people follow and the relationship is fluid? Do we really know how to be on equal footing with our partner? Or do we have to keep recreating the same power structures? Yes, it's sometimes more simple when one person makes the decisions, but in a symbiotic, collaborative union, can't we make decisions together?

According to the power structures we are familiar with, we can understand the dichotomy of leaders and followers. If we talk about a more active woman (follow) in the dance, the assumption is often that she will take over; people even offer to switch the embrace (the guy switches to the left arm wrapped around the woman). Some women learn to lead in order to have more control.

[50] The "talking stick" approach is useful when you first start toying with the idea of sharing the conversation, especially if the conversation you are used to is more like a monologue. It can help you become more aware of opportunities to speak and remind you to be attentive and listen. However, the goal is to move past this, to grow out of the training wheels and develop a sensitivity to each other that allows for a more fluid exchange of emotions and ideas and energy.

We talk about equality, but the real challenge is conceiving of a partnership in which two people can both lead and follow, listen and talk, be free to express themselves, yet attentive enough to each other to understand what each person needs, and willing to work together to move together. The real challenge is figuring out how to coexist without reenacting and reinventing the same ole power structures.

Who's the Leader?

Since I have seen the possibility of a union in which both members are active participants, I relish the opportunity to dance this way. I love being active in the dance. But since it's not taught much, I usually have to start slow and try different tactics to create these opportunities for myself. When I "put it on 'em" a little stronger, on men or leads who are not used to this type of interaction in the tango embrace, I generally get either an aggressive response or a passive response.

The aggressive response is along the lines of: stopping in the middle of the dance and saying "if you want to lead, just tell me" or they'll smirk and call it "back-leading"[51] or they'll outright call me a "rebel." These leads see it as the lead's role to call the shots and the follow's role to listen and submit – "follow." One man said of the "best follow he's ever danced with," she's a great follow because "If I don't lead it, even a *boleo*, she doesn't do it" and his son commented, "I have enough musicality for the both of us" (for him and his partner). These leads are ready to fight for their lead role. But really, you think you can lead a woman to step on a beat without her listening to the music and participating? The way the woman listens to the music and how she feels doesn't matter in the dance?

---

[51] *back-leading*: Can we use other terms for this, please? There are others, like "proposing" or "inviting" a movement. To me, "back-leading" implies that one is "forward-leading" or leading like it's supposed to be done, progressing, and the other is doing something backward, primitive, unnatural. If a follow's ideas in the dance are "back-leading," are we really acknowledging her part in the relationship? It sounds a little like saying she's "talking back." Maybe that's not what people mean when they say it, but words are important.

Another man said, "If I take a woman for a drive in *my* car, she shouldn't grab the wheel" and "If I've been talking for 10 minutes and she hasn't said anything and all of a sudden, she interrupts me —" If you've been talking by yourself for 10 minutes, maybe it's time that someone interrupted you. Wouldn't that be a lot more interesting? Come on, you're seriously so into your own monologue that no one else can speak? Or is it that you're just uncomfortable with the possibility of not knowing what will happen and relinquishing control makes you nervous?

The passive response is a little more difficult to detect: there's no initial aggression and repulsion of the idea. Instead, the lead begins to take a submissive role and in some cases, might even become less present physically (and emotionally) in the dance. He takes on the role of listening to such an extent that he becomes passive in the dance. This is a result of our dichotomy of leader-follower. *So, if I'm not leading,* he says to himself, *I'm following.* Women also do this: they switch roles from follower to leader (or they just lead). We can conceptualize our role as a leader or a follower, even the fluid lead-follow exchange of roles, yet, to have both people leading and following simultaneously, or just "being" together in a union, is harder to grasp.

If the leader stops dancing, I mean keeps moving but is no longer present and active in the dance, it's like saying, *Ok, you have the floor* and then walking away; does it matter that you've handed over the talking stick if you aren't there to listen? Just as follows should listen rather than anticipate and assume they know what you want, to maintain a fluid connection, leads must do the same when the follow proposes something. Don't "help" her; just be present and responsive to what she is asking of you. She might not be changing direction, just changing the quality of the movement you led. Let her do the work to change direction or whatever she is asking for. Just be there to listen to what she has to say.

One doesn't have to be less for their partner to be more. You can both be more active in the dance, and it actually becomes easier to do so the more you work together and balance each other out. You give her ideas and create opportunities for her and she takes them and then some, and you build off each other. The idea is that both of you speak and both of you listen. You do things together rather than one after the other; you blend as one.

A Reciprocal Relationship

A woman being active in the dance is not a challenge to the man's masculinity – he matters in the dance. It's a manifestation of her femininity, of herself. As in any endeavor where the objective is to work together, it only makes sense if he's there to receive and acknowledge her and participate, too.

Known for their manner of conversing with each other, Javier Rodriguez explains that at first Geraldine taught him and taught him and taught him and he was receiving information. Then they got to a point where they could exchange ideas.[52] It doesn't matter who teaches who; the result is that you end up having more to offer each other and being able to understand one another better. Why limit yourself with the thought that the man has to control everything? Why put that pressure on yourself? Let the woman speak. And listen, really listen. Each time you dance, you'll learn something about how your bodies intertwine.

She wants to play a little? Play along. Give her what she wants. Why not? As a lead, you can learn new moves from your partner if you move with her when she invites you to. Since it's a reciprocal relationship, by closely observing what she needs from you to make a movement work, you can learn to lead it yourself. There are endless opportunities to learn from each other and create things together.

---

[52] Geraldine Rojas and Javier Rodriguez in *La Confitería Ideal: The Tango Salon,* BBC 4 Documentary, 2005.

modern man

I'm a strong, independent, modern woman; I need a strong, modern man.

Why "strong"? Because in this modern society where women are equal and men are struggling to understand where that puts them, strength of character is what matters. Letting your woman shine doesn't take anything away from you – it doesn't make you weak and definitely doesn't make you less of a man. The modern man is confident enough in himself not to feel threatened by the power of those around him; he can recognize and appreciate the beauty of a strong woman without feeling small. Because the union of two people is not a mathematical equation; the one entity created by two people has no limits. There is no negative. The parts add to each other rather than taking away. We both shine brighter when we celebrate each other's light.

A New Flavor of Chocolate

Muñequita de alambre – Wire doll

Tango isn't about finding someone who does all the steps right, by the book, just like your favorite teacher told you. Tango is about finding someone who understands you, who can listen to you and embrace you and speak a language that you understand, too. If we could design our very own "perfect" partner, our *muñequita de alambre* (wire doll)[53] and shape it just the way we want, we would soon realize that even a wire doll that we shape ourselves is not nearly as fun as a flesh and blood person to interact with.

I want someone who can do more than just mirror me,[54] someone who can add to my dance. The agonizing beauty of it is that I'm not capable of creating this person myself. If I were to design him, he would be limited by my imagination. But the person I seek is shaped by experiences unique to him, someone who brings another perspective that enriches our union and makes it better than I could ever imagine.

---

[53] "La muñequita de alambre" is an exercise Rodolfo Dinzel uses in his Seminars on Improvisation in Tango, 2009.

[54] Inspired by a conversation with Luz Castineiras, February 2011.

A few extra steps

March 2010

It was a *milonga,*[55] which involves lots of fun little intricate steps. I like milongas. And when I get really into dancing a milonga, sometimes I lose myself a little and do a few extra steps, punching to the beat or playing with the melody. This sometimes goes with what the man's doing, but sometimes I find myself on my own. And when that happens, I usually apologize.

I've heard many responses to this situation, but when the milonga ends, Stefan says, "I don't mind those little moments. We just have to find a way to get back to moving together, to get back to the conversation."

With those two sentences, he gave me permission to try things, to play, to be free. He gave me permission to be me. He took the opportunity to hear the music the way I hear it, to be sensitive to what I feel and need. Instead of getting frustrated and suppressing my creativity, he embraced my excitement and opened doors for me to grow. His words empowered me to seek ways to channel my energy in order to connect better with him, to share it with him. Instead of trying to anchor me down, he let me fly and asked me to take him along.

---

[55] *milonga* – in this case, it's the dance

Come to the table with more than just a fork and a knife

"Come to the table with more than just a fork and a knife," my friend Chiken[56] said – you've got to bring something to the table.

And tango is no exception. I've heard women say things like, *well, if the lead doesn't do this* or *his musicality isn't that "good."* This puts a lot of pressure on the guys and they put pressure on themselves, too. But tango takes two. That means that, in pretty much any way I can think of looking at the dance, it cannot be done without the participation of both people. In any partnership, one person cannot be solely responsible – neither for the good nor the bad, nor for making it work. It's an act of two people. No matter how hard you try, you can't keep a relationship going on your own, and even if you want the other person to put in all the effort, you still have to meet him somewhere in the middle.

The idea that one should, or rather, has the opportunity to, bring something substantial to the table is not limited to musicality, nor to tango – Chiken and I were talking about potential significant others. If you are partners, you both have the privilege of bringing all that you are to the table.

---

[56] Arvin Manahan – We call each other "Chiken," like "chicken" but without the second "C." There's a story to it, but you'd have to ask one of us in person.

Play with your feet

Play with your feet. Liberate your legs. Experiment.

Accessories are beautiful, but if you put all of your earrings on at the same time, it could be a bit overwhelming. True, you need to be careful not to over spice your dish, but that doesn't mean you have to be afraid to touch the spices. Learning to cook with spices involves some experimentation – you might over spice a little here or there, but you'll eventually find a balanced taste that works for you. Part of that process is just trying it out.

Don't be afraid to go wild and crazy with a ballet bar, a chair, a wall. Dance like no one is watching. Put on some music and play on your own. When we grow up, we get so caught up with our "lives" sometimes that we forget how to play. Play with your feet, play by yourself and enjoy your own interpretation of the music. Play with the qualities of movement, the speed, the shapes, linear and circular; let your feet do the talking.[57]

When you dance with a partner it's no longer just about how you and your pretty feet interpret the music, but that doesn't mean you have to stop playing. As you dance, feel for pauses where you can add something in. The slower you dance together, the better – you'll have more time to try new things. Use your embellishments and the quality you give your steps as you transfer your weight from one leg to another to accentuate certain parts of the music, to express what you feel. As you get more comfortable with your partner and with yourself and your freed legs, let him know when you need a little more time.

Don't be afraid to play, because playing with your feet is part of developing your personal style. Like Jennifer

---

[57] Eladia Córdoba said, "The free leg speaks," 2011.

Bratt says, no half-hearted or timid embellishments; put yourself out there.[58] The first few times you try something new, it might feel awkward, but fake it till you make it. Put a little attitude into your movements, act the part, and soon your confidence will catch up.

---

[58] Jennifer Bratt, "Tango Embellishments," www.close-embrace.com/tangoembellishments.html.

Tigress

Once in a while, you come across someone on the same frequency as you. The other dances are nice, but you know what I'm talking about. It's like the difference between good conversation and conversation that enthralls you, that you lose track of time because of. It's that incredible connection, so rare that it seems impossible. And it can happen at any given time – it can take you completely by surprise. Someone can bring something out of you that you didn't even know you had in you. And once you've had it, you want more. "Like sex," says Máximo of tango as we stand on the corner of Corrientes and Lambaré, "you don't know what you're missing until you experience it, but once you've experienced it, you want more and more."

When energies meet, sometimes the combination is explosive. Sometimes, together, you create something electric. Fire:

> As we played with our feet and our movements
> resonated through our bodies and back into the ground,
> I felt the tigress in me roar.[59]

[59] My Facebook status the day after one such encounter

A new flavor of chocolate

"Want to dance?" he had asked and then hesitated: "I don't know if I'd dance this music with someone I've never danced with before." The DJ was playing Pugliese. I love Pugliese.

I looked up from picking at chopped cheeses, blueberries, and crackers. "You know, I don't know how much I believe in the music being difficult. Let's just try it. We'll go slow." And I coaxed him onto the dance floor.

Maybe it's the notion that the man has to be responsible for the musicality of the pair. That if he is, he might be hesitant to dance a more "complicated" tango with someone he hasn't test-driven to see how she responds. But if the woman can hold her own and contribute or if we make the musicality together, then it's up to both of us to make it happen and to make "us" work.

"I like the way you hear the music," he said after the first tango. We finished the Pugliese set, then some *milongas* neither of us knew really well, and then some *nuevo*[60] music.

Although I'm all for comfort, sometimes it pays to take a risk, step outside your comfort zone, step onto the dance floor with someone you have yet to discover. You might be pleasantly surprised with what you create together. I really wanted to dance to Pugliese and I was visiting from out of town, so no one knew me. I'm glad that he took a chance on me and trusted me, and I think he was, too…

"Dancing with you is like discovering a new flavor of chocolate I didn't know existed," he said to me. This guy knows how to talk to the ladies.

---

[60] *milonga* and *(tango) nuevo* – as in the genres of music

In the "Mecca" of Tango

Walk With Me to Tango Practice

Since I've decided to take the elevator down, not up (I take the stairs), I pull the handle of the hinged door toward me and then slide the accordion-style inner door open. I have to make sure that I shut both doors well, because if I don't, pushing the button labeled "PB" produces no effect. When I reach the *planta baja* (which most buildings have here – a street level upon which sits the first floor), I sigh and open up my purse again because I need the key to let myself out and I'm used to just being able to exit a building at my whim.

A right out the door and I walk up Muñiz, which becomes Yatay after crossing Avenida Rivadavia. All the street names change on the other side of Rivadavia. My route takes me under the bridge with the railroad tracks, along a one-way street (many of those around), through a quiet neighborhood, past people washing the sidewalks outside their stores or sweeping to keep things tidy. Along the way, I peer into the windows of small bakeries with their rows of pastries called *facturas* and *empanadas*, *empanadas*, and more *empanadas* (pastries filled with usually savory but sometimes sweet deliciousness). I decide to stop at one of the fruit and vegetable shops (*verdulerías,* which sometimes have meat, too), and leave with a bag containing two bananas and an apple for 2 pesos. With the exchange rate as it is now (3.6 *pesos argentinos* to the USD in March 2009), my purchase costs me less than 60 cents USD. Not bad.

I cross Avenida Corrientes, pass the Salsera club and tennis courts with crisp white lines painted in red dirt, pass the big grocery store Jumbo, cross Guardia Vieja and arrive at Rocamora, where I take a left. I swear the drivers here tend to steer toward pedestrians rather than veering away, so crossing Estado de Israel is a bit risky. Assuming I've made it across, I pass a small cafe called Camila on the corner (where the brownies aren't as good as I'd hoped, but the atmosphere is nice and fresh-squeezed orange juice is available) and I'm on Jufre. Past Marcelo's small corner eat-in or take-out *parrilla* (grill) where we tango students often gather to share french-fries and a *cerveza* (beer, often Quilmes), about half a block past it, I reach the narrow wooden door in a white stucco wall that leads down a long open air walkway.

Stepping across the tiles behind the unmarked entrance, I begin to hear the faint notes of a tango just beginning to play and imagine that as I turn the corner, I will encounter pairs of dancers beginning to embrace as they become acquainted with the rhythm and the melody and their legs begin gracefully gliding across the old wooden floor of one of the two small square rooms as they lose themselves in the music and the feeling of their mutual embrace.

Salir a la cancha: Learn by doing

> *Como las piedras en las orillas del río se pulen con el tiempo, nos pulimos en la cancha, en la pista de baile, en la vida.*
>
> Like the stones on the banks of a river smoothed by water over time, our rough edges are smoothed out on the field, on the dance floor, in life.

There's nothing like practice. Alejandra Testi told a man in the class she was teaching, "You need something that I can't give you: confidence. *Hay que salir a la cancha* – you have to get out on the field." Confidence comes from the comfort of knowing you've been there before, of having experiences to draw on to inform your present. You have to put in time, get experience: put miles on your tango-odometer, says Gary Fadling. It's like the difference between studying and working, doing internships, volunteering; the difference between talking about it and doing.

No, time does not equal skill. As if one year is the same for one person as for another, people often ask: how long have you been dancing? It's so relative. Each of us is different. We each have a different background that we bring to learning anything. Whether we practice every day or take one class per week, everyone learns at a different pace. That being said, although it does not equal wisdom nor does it equal knowledge or skill, experience is a good teacher.

Theory is good, like *dulce de leche,*[61] I told Javi one day, but if you eat a whole container of it all at once, it can

---

[61] *dulce de leche* – like dense caramel; sugar and milk cooked for hours

make you sick. It's good in moderation. There's something about sitting on the sidelines and observing or dizzying yourself with theory and rhetoric that just isn't the same as actually experiencing it yourself. Since tango you have to learn to feel, you become more sensitive with time and practice. By dancing, you figure out what feels more comfortable and maybe what you can leave out. You realize, 'Oh, he wanted a *gancho* there!' – and the next one is smoother and the next one after that more confident. If you learn through your own process of trial and error and trial, you retain so much more than if someone tells you exactly how to do things; it's more organic.

One day, I asked Rodolfo Dinzel for some feedback and he just said, *"Si caminan solos, déjalos caminar* – If they're walking on their own, let them walk." It was just the affirmation I needed to keep walking, to keep exploring. Sometimes there's no need to say much; all you need is to be reassured that you're on the right track. Sometimes we preoccupy ourselves so much with getting things "right" or getting the basics down before we start playing, that we stall and wait and set unnecessary checkpoints on the road for ourselves – just start the ball rolling, already!

The other student replied, *"Necesito pulirme* – I need to polish myself."

"¿Viste que las piedras en las orillas del río son suaves? Es que se pulen mientras les pasa el agua. – Have you noticed how the rocks on the banks of a river are smooth? That's because over time, the water polishes them. You've got to jump in the river. – *Hay que meterse en el río,"* I philosophized.

My first milonga: Salon Caning on a Monday Night

Someone told me to go to Caning on a Monday night for my first ever *milonga*. Who? I don't remember, but I do remember what happened. Salon Caning gets very crowded on Monday nights. The space is big, but the square dance floor is not so large. It's not for the soft-at-heart. I remember my friend Catrina, who was leading quite a bit, small in stature, but a tough cookie. She had to fight for space on the floor. It's really not all that bad, but just know it gets crowded. And if it's your first ever milonga, it can be a little intimidating.

Whether I was intimidated at first, I can't really remember, but the guys I danced with were tense and uptight and upset with the fact that I had no clue what I was doing. I was trying my best to "follow" them and remain upright!

Two men asked me to dance that night.

The first one stopped throughout the tango and yelled, "If you don't follow me, we can't dance!"

I tried to explain to him that after only two weeks of dancing tango, I was trying my very best. Trying. I was trying to stay in front of him – that was my reference point – and trying not to fall over on the dance floor in my *Comme-il-faut*s.[62] The last thing I wanted was to not "follow" him.

"You rebellious young kids!" he huffed.

---

[62] *Comme il faut* is a popular brand of tango shoes – these were 9cm heels.

The second guy danced some *cumbia* with me during a break between tangos and then a tango. He laughed at me and handed me his business card for classes.

Every milonga after that was easy.

Mi "Novio" de la Milonga

There was this guy who I always danced with in the *milongas*. I looked forward to dancing with him as I got ready to head out the door. You know, that guy who makes you feel so safe and contained and beautiful. I'd melt in his arms. He would ask me to dance and I'd gladly accept, nod with a smile, stand up and meet him on the dance floor. As soon as I leaned toward him and he wrapped his arms around me, my eyes closed and I was his.

I'd tell him how much I liked dancing with him – I don't hold back compliments. But the beaming smile stretched across my face was probably enough without any need for words.

When he had first started dancing tango, he said, the sequence he was executing was the most important thing. He'd bump his partners into people without much concern. But later he realized that taking care of his partner was more important than any sequence of steps.

Thank you, I told him, because I really felt like he was attentive and careful with me and my well-being.

I called him my *"novio"*[63] of the milonga because I felt a connection with him and a comfort that comes from familiarity and the building of trust. With him, I could feel safe on any dance floor. He'd gather me in his arms and I'd close my eyes and breathe and relax, so much so that once in a while, when I'd open my eyes, I'd be convinced that someone had turned the room around, that the door was supposed to be on the other side and the bar had gotten all mixed up.

---

[63] boyfriend

Un sueño

No sé si es porque nos apuramos,
porque me perdí en tu abrazo,
porque me girabas por un mundo
que me parecía algo que había soñado,
si es porque no estoy lista ni dispuesta para entregarme,
no sé que me pasa
ni porque.
Sólo sé que quiero frenar un poco,
a ver si en la lentitud descubrimos algo
que en la corrida no se nota
o si de verdad es un sueño que no se va a cumplir.

A dream

I don't know if it's because we took it too fast,
because I got lost in your embrace,
because you spun me across a world
that seemed to be something I had dreamed of,
or if it's because I'm not ready to let go
and give myself to you.
I don't know what's going on with me,
nor do I know why.
I know only that I want to slow down a little,
to see if in slow motion we discover something
that at full speed we can't perceive,
or if the truth is that it's all just a dream that will never be.

"la Moldava"

The Buenos Aires tango scene is an amazing mix of people from all over the world. I remember on one particular night I danced with several Argentinean men, including my "ex-*novio* de la milonga," a German man, an Italian man, and a man from San Diego.

But I'm the only Moldovan person here, as far as I know. And because there are so many people from all over the world here, people often ask me where I'm from. Every time I tell them, they say "What?" Not "where," but "what." When we dance again later, they say, "You're that girl from that strange country, right?" or they'll know I'm from Moldova and not remember my name.

Since there are lots of people known as "el Chino," "el Ruso," "el Turco" here – and Horacio started calling me "Moldavia" – I decided to call myself "la Moldava." It's where I was born and most people don't even know it exists. So when people ask me where I'm from, I always say Moldova and then the U.S., just to put Moldova on the map.

The international language of tango

One night at Practica X, a guy invited me to dance with a *cabeceo*.[64] I smiled and nodded back. As he approached, I stood. We faced each other. He offered his left hand; I accepted with my right. I wrapped my left arm around his back and he wrapped his right around mine and we danced. We danced a whole tango without exchanging a word. An unspoken agreement between two people to convene for the purpose of sharing an embrace.

When the song ended, he asked me, *"¿De dónde eres?"*

And as I replied, "Moldova," I was already prepared to follow it up with the usual: "It's a small country between Romania and Ukraine."

But this man spoke to me in Romanian!

It took me a few seconds to get my bearings. His name was Lucianu, and it turned out that there was a large group of twenty or so Romanians with him in Buenos Aires.

That's how I found out that there's tango in Romania. And that – through the physical language of tango – you can connect with someone without even knowing that you share a common spoken language. You can connect via the music, via the embrace, with people that you might never speak with or come in contact with otherwise, people from all walks of life, speaking all kinds of languages, with all kinds of stories. All speaking tango.

---

[64] A *cabeceo* is a way of making eye contact to invite someone to and to accept an invitation to dance.

The "Mecca" of Tango

Buenos Aires is the "Mecca" of Tango – the world center. It is likely that in a night of dancing at the more mainstream *milongas*, you will dance with many people who are not even from Buenos Aires. People from all over the world come here to hone their skills, to learn about tango the way the *porteños*[65] do it, to share an embrace that feels nostalgic, that, whether near or far from home, somehow feels like home.

[65] People from the port city of Buenos Aires are known as *porteños*.

Medialunas en la Viruta

In big cities, we rush past each other without even looking, without even acknowledging each other's presence.

I used to go to the gym, attend my yoga or pilates class, say "thank you" to the teacher and walk to my car. But then I made some friends in Marisa's step aerobics class and it became more than just a great, sweat-drippin' workout; it became social, too. We would chat during breaks, experiment with different variations and combinations to add on to the routine, synchronize, laugh and play. Class became more human.

Tango is like that, too. It's not just about the next dance; it's about the parts in between, too, when you sit at the table and chat with a friend, tell jokes and laugh, sip on some fernet and coke, or share some *medialunas*.[66]

Of course, most of us at the *milonga* want to dance tango, but at 4:30 in the morning there aren't many things that can beat the warm, freshly-baked *medialunas* with a *café con leche* or a *submarino*[67] at La Viruta. By that point in the night, some people are even too tired to dance much, but there's no cover after 3:30am and you can trade stories about your night so far and go to sleep happy with your stomach full. It's a delicious way to end the night.

The *milonga* isn't just about dancing; it's about the human interaction. As my friend Miles Tangos said, chill out, sit yourself down, and get yourself a drink – tango for the Argentineans is social.

---

[66] *Medialunas* ("half moons") are small croissant-like pastries that are traditionally eaten for breakfast or throughout the day in Buenos Aires and much of Argentina.

[67] *Café con leche* is coffee with milk; a *submarino* is warm milk with a small bar of chocolate that you mix in.

Tango in a Living Room

Dancing is part of living. Casual, spontaneous, organic. In Buenos Aires, we'd get together at a friend's house for an *asado*[68] or a birthday party or just because, and all of a sudden chairs and tables would be pushed out of the way and people would be spinning around each other and wrapping themselves around one another. No need to look for a fancy space, fancy shoes, and a special outfit; work with what you've got.

Feel like dancing? Push the furniture out of the way, put on some music, and watch the floor come alive. You don't want to dance? Sip on some *mate*[69] or a beer or grab a glass of wine; talk, laugh, watch.

---

[68] *asado* – Argentinean barbeque

[69] *mate* – a tea drunk by many Argentineans that is often consumed communally

At the Milonga: A Sea of People Swaying Together

La milonga inspira: The milonga inspires

Sitting on the white plastic stools on the patio at the studio, I was mesmerized. Wow! Did you see that? Ooh, I like that!

Back in the day, before even embracing to dance, people knew what tango looked like. They would learn the gestures by watching their uncle or grandparents dancing in the house during family gatherings; from having seen the figures from many different angles, they already understood them.[70] In *La Confitería Ideal: The Tango Salon,* Jorge Dispari says of Geraldine that she learned the basics just by watching people dancing. He used to DJ at Sin Rumbo, a *milonga* in Villa Urquiza in Buenos Aires, and she would come along and watch; "It was easy to teach her, because she loved tango."[71] Tango is walking with

---

[70] Rodolfo Dinzel, April 9, 2010.

[71] Jorge Dispari speaks of Geraldine Rojas in *La Confitería Ideal: The Tango Salon,* BBC 4 Documentary, 2005.

style; it's in the attitude and the gestures, and that you learn by watching.

Mimicking is natural. Since we were babies, we've been observing the people around us to figure out what they are doing. But these days, when studying social dances, we rely on teachers to explain to us exactly how to do each move. Sometimes words just aren't enough. When you learn by watching and experimenting, you not only learn to do "things," you start noticing what results different strategies produce. Instead of expecting your partner to put their foot in a particular place, you feel for where your partner is actually at and adjust as necessary. You recognize how things feel in your own body. In an interview, Horacio Godoy said of his teachers: "You had to learn by watching them. One would ask, 'But how?' and they'd respond, *'Miralo, pibe'* – 'Watch, kid'."[72] When you watch, try to understand what makes it work: the "how," not just the "what." Just because no one "taught" you something, doesn't mean you can't try it.

At the studio, we'd spend a lot of time sitting on those plastic stools on the patio. We'd sip *mate* and eat cookies, chat, and watch each other dance. I remember getting ideas for things I wanted to try or seeing *gancho* after *gancho* before actually doing one myself. When we watch, we choose the elements we like most, those that resonate with us, and we integrate them into our dance. Because we learn them by trying them out, we each find a way that fits our body, we make them our own. It's a cycle that fuels itself: when we learn by watching each other, we build on our ideas and perpetuate each other's growth.

---

[72] Muriel Rébori, Interview with Horacio Godoy, *La Milonga Argentina*, Issue 51: May 2010.

El Cabeceo: The prelude to a kiss[73]

The *cabeceo* is the prelude to the dance,
that moment when you hope to get his attention
so that he might hold your gaze with his eyes
and nod his head toward the dance floor,
that moment when you don't know
if you'll dance together or not,
when you brush close to each other
and you feel each other breathe,
and you revel in the wonder
of the possibilities
of what will happen next.

---

[73] Inspired by a drink called "Prelude to a Kiss," LUCID Jazz Lounge.

"No" is not a bad word

"No" is not a bad word. Yes, it can mean rejection, humiliation, and heartbreak. But saying "yes" when you really mean and feel like saying "no" can mean lying, betrayal, not respecting yourself and what you need. Saying "no" if that is what you truly feel leaves room for the other person to find someone who actually wants to say "yes" to them and gives you the opportunity to say "yes" to someone or something else that you actually want to say "yes" to.

If you can release yourself from the pressure of feeling like you should say "yes," your no's will carry less baggage. A simple, polite, "no, thank you" or a discreet shake of the head, maybe accompanied by a smile, gets the point across. No rolling of the eyes necessary.

And if you're on the receiving end of a "no," remember that it might have nothing to do with you. Rather than worrying about rejection, worry that someone might say "yes" when what they mean is "no." Sometimes we get so caught up in the fact that we want someone to say "yes" to us that we fixate on the response "yes." We take "no" personally because we enter the situation with our expectations before us.

What if that person ends up saying "yes" just because I am so excited for them to say "yes" and not because that is actually what she wants? There's a fine line between being persistent and being overbearing. "No" can be hard to swallow, but isn't it worse to be in a situation thinking that the other person wants the same thing and then to realize they don't? It's easy to end up feeling disillusioned or hurt, but the problem might have started simply because I didn't really listen.

Then again, there are those situations when people do lie to us and tell us what they think we want to hear. This man was talking about being married to his wife for 30 years out of pity for her. He didn't want to leave her because he felt bad for her, he said. So he wasted 30 years of her life? He assumed that she wanted to be with him without telling her the whole truth? He assumed that she could not find someone who would actually want to be with her? Please don't do me that kind of favor! I'd rather wallow in the sorrow of a "no" than feel the betrayal of "no" that's disguised as a "yes."

If what you mean is "no," please, say "no." No dances out of pity or obligation. It's not fun to dance when you don't feel like it, to do anything without feeling like it. There are probably other ladies in the room who would be delighted to dance with your "no, thank you" guy. If you're not one of them, let him find them and vice versa.

And if you're asking someone to dance, please, no begging or pleading. Respect a "no" for what it is: no. If you get a lot of no's, maybe they have to do with things beyond your control. Or maybe you're the heavy-breathing, huffy-puffy guy that rubs the ladies' backs and has been known to undo a bra strap. So maybe the ladies aren't so into that.

Assuming you're not that guy, you could try paying more attention to who is inviting you to ask them to dance. Since the *cabeceo* is like a prelude to a kiss, if she does not show interest, do not continue with the kissing procedure: retreat! People often say "yes" well before you ask them. Look for those who want to dance with you.

You can't live your life lamenting the no's and second-guessing the yes's. Trust that when you ask, you will get the most honest answer the person can give you. Then the no's become more palatable and you can celebrate the yes's because they really are that: yes's.

Dear Huffy-Puffy Breathing Guy,

Tango is intimate. It involves sharing much of the surface of your body with another person. Standing chest-to-chest, cheek-to-cheek, and sometimes even hip-to-hip with someone feels safe because I know that he will touch me only in a way that relates to the dance, to the mutual agreement we've come to in order to dance this dance.[74]

But just like in any social activity, there are people who overstep the limits. If you're that huffy-puffy, deep breathing guy who takes advantage of your close proximity to a lady's body while she has entrusted herself in your arms to dance a tango, especially if you prey on the ladies newer to tango who might not know what is expected and what's acceptable, you should be ashamed of yourself. And please, please don't go around telling ladies that a pelvic thrust is "tango" and that if they don't like that, they should dance cha-cha or some other dance. True story.

If your partner is uncomfortable, it doesn't matter if "everyone else is doing it" or if it's part of your repertoire of acceptable "tango moves"; it doesn't matter who said it was ok. There's no winning an argument about how somebody feels.

---

[74] And if I *do* invite more, I don't want it to happen on the dance floor.

La pista – The dance floor

Dance floors are full of testosterone clashing with testosterone.

> One night I'm dancing at la Glorieta, a crowded outdoor *milonga.* I know that navigating the floor there is not easy, so I try to relax as much as possible to help my partner feel calmer. I breathe deep, hug him real close, caress his back, bring my cheek next to his and suddenly he stops dancing and yells out, *"¡Hijo de puta!"* – "Son of a bitch!" Seriously? *No dá.* It just doesn't fit. And if it happens to be for my protection, thanks, but no thanks.

The dance floor doesn't have to be chaotic or violent. We're just looking for a peaceful mutual existence. Collisions happen. The goal is to make them as infrequent as possible, and we each do our part to help out. When I get bumped, my lead often apologizes. I tell him that I trust him, that I know that he is trying his best to keep me safe, and I try to relax again, because that's important, too.[75]

> Then there's Oscar Pereiro who, regardless of if he caused the collision or the other lead did, apologizes and then asks me if I'm ok. He says he's won many friends this way. You have to be cool about it, *tirar buena onda,* he says. Then the other guy, who might have felt the need to get defensive even if it was actually his fault, has no choice but to be calm about it, too. Everyone's happy and we keep dancing.

---

[75] Of course, there are limits: If I feel unsafe or like my partner is being reckless with my well-being, I say "thank you" and sit down.

Tango is a popular dance. Anyone should be able to share the floor with you and deserves your respect. The point of tango is not to be "better" than someone else: *"No hay uno mejor que otro* – there isn't one guy better than another," says El Chino Perico. Yes, you can compete and see who can do the fanciest footwork, but if you're so "good" that no one else wants to dance around you, there's no one left to compete with. *"El hombre tiene que halagar al hombre, no tirarlo por abajo"* he says – "the men have to compliment each other, not pull each other down." It benefits all of us if there are more people who feel comfortable and welcome in our dancing community.

It's not a competition or a race. The dance floor is a never-ending circuit. Being a good dancer doesn't equal getting around the floor faster, there is no prize for weaving in and out of the lanes, there's no need to try to "pass" people. If the experience itself is the most important part, why does it matter how "far" you get or how fast you get there?

If the couples on the floor maintain a consistent distance between those in front of them and those behind them, things seem to run organically. It's a synchronized cycle of creating space and taking space. When there is no room to advance, they get creative and do something in place. Out of respect for the flow, people make eye contact before merging onto the floor. There are some basic codes of mutual respect to follow, says Rodolfo Dinzel: you don't bother anyone and the rest of the people don't bother you. If everyone works together, it's smooth sailing.

A sea of people swaying together

Although each couple on the floor interprets the music differently, we are a sea of people swaying together. There's a collective feeling, a frequency we tune into. When we enter the line of dance, we ride the current; we somehow synchronize with those around us. We are independent, yet bonded: individuals, yet a community.

We need each other, like dogs in a pack. I'm used to dogs meeting one-on-one, bickering and growling, when they each have to be the Alpha and the Omega and everything, all alone. But if you watch the dogs with the dog walkers in Buenos Aires, it's the most surprising thing: in a pack they get along – 10 or 12 of them. We all need to belong, like the baby hippopotamus named Owen who befriended and adopted Mzee, a 130-year-old giant tortoise, as his "mother" after being separated from his pod during a tsunami.[76] Friends come in all shapes and sizes and we all need them.

Like seaweed, those rocks in our path are there for us to bend around and adapt to; they remind us that we're seaweed and we remind them that they're rocks. The *milonga* is where people come together to dance, to feel like part of a group. It's not the same as performing on a floor by yourself or practicing alone with your partner. At the *milonga*, the point is to coexist.

---

[76] Hatkoff, Isabella, Craig Hatkoff, & Dr. Paula Kahumbu, *Owen and Mzee: The True Story of a Remarkable Friendship,"* Scholastic Press: 2006.

Like a Cat Chasing Its Tail

Back to the Basics

The first tango class I ever took, the first time I ever saw Argentinean tango, was at a club called La Viruta. They have many levels of classes going on at the same time and you can sort of place yourself. So my first tango class, I hopped into the class with the twists and turns – *ochos,* I found out they were called. The just walking, that's too easy, I told myself.

Tango is easy… and it's not. Sometimes the simplest things are the most difficult to perceive, so the fact that it's so "easy" is what makes it so elusive. I was used to dance classes based on the idea that you learn steps; the more steps you know, the better you dance. But tango doesn't work that way. It's not about the steps. Walking is the ultimate objective.

In my zest to learn "more" my first time ever seeing tango, I placed myself in the second class at La Viruta only to return two years later in search of the essence and the basics and the sophisticated channeling of energy between two people in Horacio Godoy's classes. Tango is not a linear learning process; it's spiral and circular and it can take years and many miles to realize that going "back to the basics" is what it takes to develop that other-level type of connection.

It all comes "back" to walking…

When life gives you lemons

The Facebook status post went something like this:

> when life gives you lemons, buy a bottle of tequila, says Amanda. lol! or... make lemon bars – yum!

and the comments that followed were:

> **Reggie:** when life gives you lemons you say fuck that and get a steak.
> **Me:** lol. i like that, Reggie!
> **Me:** oh and for the record, i made a steak dinner with salmon on the side, lemon juice all over it and lemon margaritas all over that dance floor. left everything i had in me at the milonga :) great dances, great company, great night!

I sat at the studio and as I looked around, I noticed that the men were pretty dramatically outnumbered by the women, and I just didn't see how the situation at hand was going to promote my growth as a dancer. One guy who I'd love to practice with was packing up to go and another one who said he'd be there that day hadn't shown up yet. I mean, in order to make significant improvements, I need to be challenged and pushed, and sitting on a plastic stool on the patio sipping *mate* for hours on end was not going to get me there. As I surveyed the faces of my fellow female dancers, each eagerly awaiting the end of the next tango to see who would be the next to leave the dance floor and swap out his dance partner by extending a hand their way, I put on a sour face and gave in to the "tango slump."

"This was bound to happen," my friend Amber analyzed, an encouraging hand on my shoulder. "You've been dancing a lot and going strong. A slump is bound to happen."

"I guess," I sighed. But after meditating on the situation for a few more moments, I stood up, grabbed the faded pink strap of my tango shoe bag and announced that I wasn't going to take this slump sitting down. "When life gives you lemons," I asserted, "make lemonade or lemon pie or… hell, eat the lemons, 'cause I like lemons." I had a plan: go to teach the English class I had that afternoon – to feed my tango addiction – and then out to dance. And that's exactly what I did. I went to the class and then stayed for the *milonga* and spent very little time warming the seat at my table. I was lucky, too: not only did I dance a lot, but all the men danced the way I liked. The night was going so well and I had such an urge to keep moving my dancing feet, that I walked the four blocks to La Viruta and danced some more – until they played "La Cumparsita"[77] and turned on the bright lights.

I went to the studio the next day and when I walked in, the ratio of women to men was 3:1. Again? This can't be happening! I got a little practice in but felt far from satisfied. When Stefan got there I was almost sure he'd ask me to dance, but he didn't. I watched the couples dancing, which I like to do, and did my stretching routine, but at the end of the day, I felt discouraged and deeper into my slump. Hang my head low? No way. I went out again that night and danced until La Viruta closed at 6:00am, walked home, and felt accomplished. It's just a slump. It'll pass, I told myself.

---

[77] "La Cumparsita" is usually the last tango of the night.

The following day I was in no big hurry to get to the studio, as I thought I knew what was in store for me there. I strolled down the street, admiring the huge red flower by Marcelo's *parrilla*. At the studio, Amber and I analyzed my slump and my relationship with tango. This is what happens, we concluded, it's like you're never satisfied. And how could you be? It's an addiction, so you always want more, right? Right.

I stretched, took deep breaths, meditated a little. At one point I made eye contact with Stefan and we walked to the dance floor, embraced, and began to walk together. He gave me pointers and I felt more encouraged. We connect well, we speak. Afterward, as he got his stuff together to head out, we talked.

"I was kind of having a down period the last few days here at the studio," I confessed.

"Yes, I noticed that you seemed a bit distant." His response took me by surprise.

"You could tell? I mean, there were so many women and I just felt like I wasn't dancing very much," I tried to explain.

"You know, when I first came to the studio, I felt very welcomed, but some friends of mine who came later said that they didn't get the same feeling. They paid the fee, but they felt like no one approached them and took care of them. When I asked Rodolfo [Dinzel] about this, he said, 'What can I do if people don't want something?' You have to think about what you want and go for it," Stefan said. "If you want to dance, just ask me and I'll dance with you. If you want advice, ask for it."

And that's when I realized that my "proactive" attitude, my not-going-to-take-this-sitting-down mentality, was all to counter the energy I was putting out myself. Yes, it's true that there were more women than men a couple of days in a row, but who would want to dance with me if I'm in a self-proclaimed slump. I exacerbated the situation myself. We all go through slumps, so just ride the downward curve of the wave. Don't fight it and tense up, because you'll sink even lower. Soon there'll be another wave to carry you up. The next time you find yourself with some lemons, I'd recommend sippin' on a lemon drop.

The Ups and the Downs

Sometimes life does give you lemons and sometimes they really are sour. And when you really feel sad, you might have to shed a few tears or laugh at the absurdity of the universe. Life isn't always rosy; you have to live the ups and the downs. If you're already on the rollercoaster, it will inevitably go down. There's no getting off now, so just surrender to it. Let go, because fighting it can make it harder to come up the other side. And up the other side it will go and down again, because life is full of ups and downs.

Sometimes you have to go backward to go forward…

I was playing Solitaire. In order to get all the cards out and finish the game, I had to use some cards that I had already put on top of the aces. To proceed, although it seemed counterintuitive, I had to go backward.

You sometimes have to go backward in tango, too – or it might seem like backward – to more basic concepts in order to be able to understand and execute the more complex ones. You always return to more simple concepts and when you're really experienced, those are the ones that matter most, people say.

There is no Checklist

Tango is fluid and alive. It lives in us. There is no checklist of skills you've mastered so you've learned tango. It's organic and subtle in all its intricacies. The journey is the search and it can be never-ending. If you choose to see the end, you'll find it; if not, the possibilities are infinite.

"This, I know how to do," said my friend. "Easy."

The actual steps themselves weren't complicated. But that was exactly the issue. Because he "knew" how to do it, he couldn't feel what was missing. He was just doing, but tango isn't about doing; it's about being.

Not like building a desk

Many people approach tango like building a desk: they want a step-by-step process that leads them to a clear end result.

But tango is about the process, not the end result. Tango is about the search, the discovery, the yearning for more. Tango is about pushing the boundaries from within, in a way that might be imperceptible to anyone else around, sometimes even to your partner. Sometimes you even surprise yourself.

It's about finding yourself, and like the cat chasing its tail, it takes a long time.

Those guys who know "everything"

You've danced with those guys who know "everything" – you know who they are. They're the ones who try to pack in as many complex combinations as possible before the *chun (chun)* at the end of the song. And you probably don't want to dance with them again.

Like a good speech, it's the "How" not the "What"

Don't chase the music and sweat displaying all of your tango vocabulary – it's not about how many words you know or how fast you can say them.

"Tango is like a speech," says Geoffré Dominessy, "it's about how you use the words you know." Read the crowd. Engage your partner. Feel how her body responds to you.

Great speakers stimulate the crowd and ride the current. They wait for the clapping to subside, just long enough, but not so long as to lose the flow of energy. They manage the momentum and use it to their advantage, knowing when to add to it, when to coast, when to slow down. They hold the crowd breathless with the resonance of their words in each dramatic pause. When they feel the energy building they might choose to repeat a word an extra time, just to emphasize the point that has the crowd invigorated, just to let them know they hear them.

Take Your Sweet Time

Simplicity

Ironically, the handwritten first draft of this entry was anything but simple. That's because sometimes the simplest things are the most difficult to capture. You grasp and grasp at mouthfuls of words that slip through your fingers like sand, and talk in circles to say something that you could express with a simple touch. When people first start dancing tango, they often see "moves" and "things" and think that that's what they need to do (a lot of) to dance tango.

But *todo lo que brilla no es oro* – everything that glitters is not gold. The important things aren't always things we can see. Most people know hundreds of figures and only dance with seven, says Rodolfo Dinzel. *"No es hacer muchas cosas grandes; es hacer pocas cosas con grandeza,"* he says – "It's not about doing lots of big things; it's about doing few things with grandeur." Yet many people keep seeking figures.

We are a results and output-oriented society. We want things measureable and clear and fast. We detach ourselves from the journey by constructing highways and byways and helicopter landing pads to transcend the reality that exists along the way. More is better, speed and efficiency is what counts.

But how do you measure your grandma's love or a smile on a child's face or the warm feeling of a hug or the emptiness when someone leaves? Tango has to do with the things we can't quantify, the things we struggle to put into words and write entire books about, things that are so simple that we don't know how to express them. Tango has to do with choosing, because more is not always better and the little things do count and if you have less of something then you really have to be picky. Because it's not about how much I can grasp in the breadth of my arms and it's not about something I can put into words, and you know what I mean without me even having to say anything.

Make all the movements count

I remember Rodolfo Dinzel telling a student that each and every movement is important and that one's dance should reflect this.

Instead of moving as if to get it over with, put importance into each detail. Make all the movements count, like in chess. And that sometimes means choosing quality over quantity, because if you try to cram all the steps you know into one tango, some part of your dance will suffer. Dance as though each moment is a little piece of your life that you'll never get back.

Momentos de Espera

"Hoy, todo es rapidez y descartable,"[78]
vamos por la vida figura tras figura, corriendo.
A veces corremos tanto que ni respiramos.

Pero en el tango se valora el no hacer como el hacer,[79]
la quietud como el movimiento,
el silencio como la palabra.

Hay que buscar momentos de espera,
"resetear la maquina,"
y mientras tanto, "cargar energía"
para volver a pisar otra vez.
Y hay que pisar con ganas,
trasladarse con ganas y parar con ganas,
no seguir corriendo atrás del tiempo fuerte o del compás
o porque alguien me dijo que tengo que hacerlo.
Tampoco es pausar porque me dijeron que hace falta.

Es buscar sentir y escuchar
y hacer lo que realmente tengo ganas de hacer.
Así cada movimiento queda sincero,[80]
así cada movimiento vale más
por el tiempo que lo esperé
y cada pausa es un regalo
de estar abrazado.

---

[78] Rodolfo Dinzel, April 7, 2010.
[79] Inspired by a conversation with Daniel Ledesma, April 23, 2011.
[80] Horacio Godoy, April 2011: "resetear la máquina," "cargar energía," y movimientos sinceros en vez de movimientos organizados, como mentiras.

A veces hacemos cosas por la angustia de no hacer nada,
por la angustia de quedarnos quietos;
decimos palabras sin pensarlas,
para llenar el silencio.
Pero haciendo "cosas"
cedemos la libertad de eligir
porque el moverse se siente tan lindo
por el hecho de no moverse,
y parar se agradezca
por interrumpir la corrida,
por un momento y la oportunidad
de respirar,
de buscar tierra,
de buscar al otro,
de encontrarme con mí mismo otra vez.

Moving just to move

Sometimes we move just to move,
because we don't know how to live the stillness.
We keep running from one appointment to another,
we dance sequence after sequence,
because we don't know how to stop,
because we don't know
how to just be.
So we do "things" to fill up time,
we make jokes to fill the silences,
we speak empty words.

But each movement grows more beautiful
in the excitement of its anticipation,
and each pause is a chance
to celebrate just being in each other's company.
Seek to move because you feel it
and to pause when it seems right,
not because somebody said so,
but because you feel compelled
to do so.

Because in doing just to do,
we forsake the liberty of choosing;
we become prisoner to the clock.
Because action is a release
and pauses are a chance to gather energy;
because motion takes on value
when juxtaposed with tranquility;
because we appreciate the pauses
for the fact that they are a contrast to the running,
for the opportunity to breathe,
to ground ourselves,

to revisit the connection with our partner,
to find ourselves once again.

Life in cruise control

Sometimes life becomes so routine that we overlook the details and get from point A to point B without even knowing how we got there.

This guy once said to me after half a tango, *"Me duermo la siesta* – I feel like I'm taking a nap," as in bored. Really? Sometimes you just don't click with someone, so neither the little details nor the big things work. But "bored" is a cop-out, an excuse, a lack of ownership for your own existence. Please remember that connection takes two and that if you're "bored," it means you're part of creating and perpetuating that boredom.

Play with the textures of the music, the relationship between our bodies, the endless combinations and permutations of the interlacing of our souls. Invade my space, take it. Let me feel your pulse, let me feel that you're alive through the tiny fluctuations in your movements as you adapt and respond to the yearnings of my being.

This car doesn't come in automatic.

Take your sweet time

When you're new at something, the excitement is in getting "there," whatever the objective is.

But as you mature through experience, you start asking yourself, What am I rushing for? And it stops being about getting to the next milepost or completing tasks to cross off your list. You start savoring every second and living those "in between" parts.

And you start taking your sweet time.

The Things You Can't See

That Invisible Connection

Some things you can only see when you change the lighting,
some things you can only see from a distance,
some things you have to get real, real close to see.

And then there are those things
that you can't see no matter how close you get;
you can only feel them.

Ver de lejos; sentir de cerca

A veces tienes que alejarte para ver, tomarte un tiempo. Pero como no te puedes ver bailando, ni te puedes alejar, hay que sentir – no queda otra – tomar conciencia de ti mismo. Y así el otro puede tomar conciencia de ti también. Sólo tú puedes sentir lo que se siente dentro de la pareja. Nadie te puede aconsejar como estar o encontrarte o entenderte con otra persona – o sí te pueden dar consejos, pero tú tienes que tomar la decisión, porque nadie sabe mejor que tú.

See from a distance; feel right here

Sometimes you have to back up to see, take your time to see. But since you can't see yourself in the act of dancing tango and you can't distance yourself, you have to feel – there's no other way. You have to become conscious of yourself. And in doing so, you help your partner become conscious of you, too. Just like in a relationship, only you can feel what it feels like between the two of you, on the inside. Nobody can tell you how to be with or build a connection with or understand another person – and if they do give you advice, only you can decide what to do, because no one knows what you feel better than you.

Tango is Ephemeral

While walking around a garden with my Grandpa Carl admiring flowers, he recited this poem to me:

Intr-o grădină	In a garden
Intr-o grădină lâng-o tulpină văzui o floare de farmec plina s-o rup, se strică s-o las, mi-e frică că vine altul şi mi-o rădică	In a garden I saw a flower full of magic if I pick it, it dies if I leave it, I fear that someone else will come along and take it from me

– Goethe interpreted by Ienăchiţă Văcărescu

As soon as I try to see what it looks like in the mirror, I lose the connection with my partner. Videos fall short of capturing the energy. Pictures are just static snapshots of a dynamic, fluid motion.

When I studied in Rome for a quarter my sophomore year of college, I spent much of my time behind a camera. I wanted to capture everything. But that's impossible, I realized, and because I was so busy trying to "record" it in pictures that I haven't looked at in years, I didn't always make the most of my experience; I wasn't always truly present.

Tango, like the flower in the garden, like our transient human existence, is ephemeral. It's fleeting, impermanent. Only you and I know what we feel in our embrace, yet only those who see us can admire the shapes we create. There's no use trying to grasp it; as soon as you do, it disappears.

Tango is and isn't. It was and wasn't. There is no past, no future, just now and now and… now.

Oh, the paradoxes!

You must let go to have more possibilities
relax to control
be soft to be strong
be clear and decisive
yet listen and be perceptive.
You must use a little tension, but not much force
embrace, without smothering
trust, but not blindly
find elegance in subtlety
and sophistication in simplicity.
The more you progress, the less complicated it becomes…

Feel to move rather than move to feel[81]

> They say that *"el tango es un sentimiento que se baila"* – "tango is an emotion that you dance."

"Hay días que no sirvo para nada. Estoy como toda floja," one woman says – "Some days I'm not good for anything. I'm all loose," and she sways her torso around from side to side to show the disconnection. But it's not that you aren't good for anything. If we dance our emotions, if we dance what we feel, obviously our emotions change so our dance does, too. We are feeling to move rather than moving to feel; if you don't feel what you feel, how can you dance what you feel?

She adds, "It seems like some women who are more experienced dancers can control this better" and thus keep their highs and lows less extreme. The highs and lows will always be there and you might even feel them more intensely as you develop this connection with yourself.[82] Becoming *la dueña de tu propio cuerpo* – the master of your own body means learning to let your emotions flow; it means not getting upset about being upset and learning to channel this energy into your dance so that you stay connected with yourself even when you don't feel 100%. You can't hide from your emotions. Words lie, but in tango, your body does the talking and your body doesn't lie.[83]

If we move because we feel, if we dance our emotions, it makes sense to connect differently with our dance

---

[81] Rodolfo Dinzel, February 15, 2010.

[82] I look at my baby niece Kera: at 5 weeks, she has no reservation about crying when she's not happy and smiling with delight – she's connected with herself with no inhibitions. May 2011.

[83] "Las palabras mienten, pero el cuerpo no," Rodolfo Dinzel, 2010.

partners on different days. No two tangos, even between the same two people, will ever be the same. As Rodolfo Dinzel explains, one can't bathe twice in the same waters of a river.

When we interact with people, we have to allow for that human fluctuation, that natural change. I'm not a robot; I can't recreate yesterday's conditions and I'm not the same person I was yesterday or even five minutes ago. All the technique and theory don't wipe away a heavy heart: they're tools to express it. Let your heart be your paintbrush,[84] speak with your feet; *"el tango te tiene que poner la piel de gallina, hermano. Si no, no va* – tango has to give you goose pimples, brother. If not, it simply doesn't work."[85]

---

[84] Inspired by the song "Vipassana" by Macklemore and Ryan Lewis, *The VS. EP* Album, 2009.
[85] Jorge Zanada, dir., *Tango Baile Nuestro,* Film. 1988.

Chocolate Nuances

"To someone who doesn't like chocolate, like me," said Rodolfo Dinzel, "it's all the same." To a chocolate connoisseur, there are infinite types of chocolate; she can perceive the subtle variations in different chocolate bars.

So it is with tango, or any discipline that you develop aptitude in: growing as a tango dancer means becoming more perceptive of the *matices* – the little nuances, the details. "When you're hungry to learn and everything is new," says Fernando Gordillo, "you eat anything. With time, you learn to choose." You begin discerning what you like and what you could skip a second helping of.

You start noticing the subtle weight changes and pick up on differences in energy and momentum and qualities of movement. The more skilled you become at perceiving these details, the greater the range of possibilities you have to play with. Tango isn't black or white. It's gray, lots and lots of different hues of gray.

Beware of the dichotomy of black and white. Nobody's simply good or bad. We define things to simplify them so that we don't have to deal with the complexity of their essence. We box them up so they're easier to categorize. If we resist the urge to label in the face of the undefined, we can appreciate the beauty of the complexity of the many nuances of each person we encounter.

Lines make us feel better, but that doesn't mean that it's better to see the world in homogenous blocks and circles rather than the intricacies of its uneven, irregular forms. It's hard to teach the gray and often hard to grasp the gray, so people resort to black and white. Extremes and absolutes are easier to work with. But easy isn't always better. Life is all about the gray. Life is about the chocolate nuances.

Te falta la mugre – Too clean

When that teacher explained to me that if I do adornments on the strong beat, I might not have enough time to get to the next movement the guy is leading, he said, "If it happens once, ok. Twice, hm…" and then he sort of implied that the said guy might choose not to dance with me again.

Since there are as many styles as people dancing tango and our personalities and sentiments inform our dance, I saw two options: 1) I conform to what the majority of the guys want so that they will ask me to dance, because I want to dance, or 2) If I plan to preserve my individuality, I have to stay strong and keep doing what I feel. Or a little bit of both. In a social environment, a little bit of compromising and bending might need to happen in order to be able to interact with the group at large. However, one of the most beautiful things about tango is that when you look at a floor full of people dancing, they all dance differently.

If I start becoming too preoccupied with dancing in a way that makes other people happy, in this case, to follow exactly what the guy is leading, exactly, exactly, I'll lose my own personal style, my individuality. If one guy doesn't ask me to dance again but others do, I can keep dancing with those who like the way I dance, no? You can't make everyone happy all the time.

Astor Piazzolla said to Miguel Angel Estrella, a famous classical musician, *"Tocás como los dioses, pero te falta la mugre* – you play like a god, but you're missing the dirt."[86]

---

[86] Astor Piazzolla quoted by Karina Louro in a conversation in March 2011. I was unable to document the direct quote, but Piazzolla was known for talking about *"la mugre"* (the grit, the dirt) – it's that little something that makes tango tango.

El tango es la mugre, es vivo, es humano porque le damos un toque de nuestra humanidad – tango is dirty, it's impure, it's alive, it's human because we put a touch of our humanity into it. *"Cuando bailamos un tango, nos prestamos el alma,"* says Rodolfo Dinzel – "When we dance a tango, we lend each other our souls."

Put yourself, your personality, in your dance. *"No hay que tener miedo de 'ensuciar' el baile,"* says Eva Wagner – "don't worry about 'dirtying' the dance." Don't hold back out of fear of disturbing or interrupting or sabotaging the plan. You are part of the tango, so you can't interrupt it by doing anything short of letting go of your partner and leaving him alone on the dance floor. You are tango.

Choices

There's lots of pressure to be good, correct, right, and so many definitions of what "right" is. We all make choices, but choices are like clothes: some fit you well, some you grow out of, and others might be better suited for a clothing exchange. And you might have to try on a lot of clothes to figure out what fits you best. But if we avoid making choices or go by someone else's rulebook, we lose ourselves. We don't have to wait for the sun to shine to feel our sunshine from within. Watch out for being so busy with being "right" and "ready" for life to happen that you miss the sunshine altogether.

We're much more similar than we are different

We have so much trouble understanding each other because we are trying so hard to interpret the products of people's desires literally that we don't really listen. We miss authenticity because we convince ourselves that copying someone or some move is "authentic." And that's when we stop being authentic ourselves. Instead of trying to read each note and phrase literally and relying on someone to tell you what's "correct," listen to it, really listen.

When you understand how the music makes you feel, how someone's touch makes you feel, how it makes you feel to see a teardrop find its way down someone's cheek, you'll be a lot closer to empathizing and understanding the composer and the musicians, the emotion in the singer's voice, the breathing of the bandoneón. When you can empathize with yourself, relating to others becomes so much easier. Tango is emotions played as notes, sung as poems, expressed through the quality of our movements. Emotions are universal.

Once we stop being so stubborn about our viewpoint, about being "right," about winning an argument, we can see how the walls that we put up between "us" and "them" really don't have to be there, that we're much more similar than we are different. When we really want to understand each other, we find a way.

As Many Tangos...

As many tangos as people who have danced tango and times they've danced[87]

In 1951, Felipe Richiardi went to La Plata[88] to play with D'Arienzo's orchestra one night. Since he didn't have the address for the venue, when he got off the train, he asked someone. "Follow the people," a man replied. Going to see D'Arienzo's orchestra was like going to a stadium to see the Boca Jr.'s play.[89] All kinds of people listened to and danced tango.

Because tango is a popular dance, in which the manner rather than the form is what counts, anyone can dance it.[90] Any Joe Shmoe can do it his own way, how he feels it. All he needs is someone who's willing to embrace him and dance with him. *"Cada uno tiene su estilo* – each one has his own style," says El Chino Perico. There are as many styles as people dancing tango: "There's good tango, bad tango, and weird tango," my friend Tony likes to paraphrase Luciana Valle, "tango I like, tango I don't like, and tango I'm not sure if I like or not." Trends depend on the individuals who dance tango – their fashion, their preferences, their social interactions with one another. You can sense different vibes in different *milongas* and in different neighborhoods. But tango is tango.

---

[87] Rodolfo Dinzel, *El Tango, una danza...,* 2008, p. 9.
[88] La Plata is a city just south of Buenos Aires.
[89] Horacio Godoy told this story during a Saturday class, April 2011.
[90] Rodolfo Dinzel, *El Tango, una danza…*, 2008, p. 13.

Since it's not a choreographed dance and you dance what you feel, adjusting to the particular circumstances each moment presents you, it's impossible to replicate. That's the richness of the dance: no two tangos are ever the same. *"Hay miles de parejas bailando, pero usted no va a ver ni una pareja que baile igual* – There may be thousands of couples dancing, but you won't see two couples dancing the same."[91]

"Tango is a *cambalache,*" says Karina Louro.

> *cambalache* – a medley, a miscellaneous
> collection; a potpourri

A *cambalache* of personalities, music, styles, clothing, ages, professions, cultures, languages. *Hay cada rana en este poso* – there are all types of frogs in this pond. And somehow it works.

---

[91] Jorge Zanada, dir., *Tango Baile Nuestro,* Film. 1988.

Una Búsqueda Eterna

El tango no es algo que aprendés y ya está. Es continuo y constante. El tango se acaba cuando terminás de buscarlo. El tango termina cuando pensás que ya sabés todo. Porque el tango fluye, como el agua, y sigue con vos o sigue sin vos, pero siempre te espera; siempre estará cuando estés listo para buscarlo.

An Eternal Search

Tango isn't something you learn and that's it. It's constant and continuous. Tango ends when you stop searching for it. Tango ends when you think you know everything there is to know. Because tango flows, like water, and it continues with or without you, but it always waits for you; it will always be there when you're ready to seek it out.

Let Your Own Light Shine

A teacher's job is to help his students gain confidence in themselves. Creating situations of dependency might seem good for your pocket short-term, but it is not good for your students – and long-term, I would argue that it's not good for you, either. The point is to get your students to stand on their own four feet.

So teach instead with the idea that your students' potential extends past your own limits; that they can surpass your capabilities. Teach your students with the expectation that they can grow beyond the boundaries of your imagination. If you assume that your students can only achieve what you know, you limit them and yourself from the very beginning.

Give unselfishly and without apprehension and it will come back to you. Give because if your students grow, you will, too. It's not always easy – you have to trust yourself. But once you stop trying to live up to the impossible role of the all-knowing, you'll realize just how much more you really know.

Don't hold back out of fear. Know that by letting your own light shine, you give others permission to do the same[92] – there's enough light for all of us. Together, we are more.

---

[92] Marianne Williamson, *A Return to Love: Reflections on the Principles of A Course in Miracles,* Harper Collins, 1992: pg.191.

On Giving out Fish

A few days after my workshop on musicality, a participant told me that at first he was kind of upset because he didn't feel like he had walked away with more material or vocabulary to interpret Piazzolla with. I said, interpret him *¡como te canta el culo!* – however the hell you feel! But he wanted fish. I told him, I'm not interested in giving out fish. When you realize that tango isn't about collecting "things," come talk to me. He had spoken about the workshops with some friends, who advised him that these might be useful concepts, but "advanced." I agree: I think they are ideas that don't have to do with what you do, but how you do it, but they are crucial from the very beginning.

He insisted that if I structured my workshops more (taught steps), more people would come, that people have different learning styles. I replied, And people have different teaching styles.

We know that the customer is not always right. The idea that since I have money, I have power, is flawed. Hugo Linares and Claudia Ubal pointed this out to me. They told me that when customers say to them, *Well, I'm paying you,* they say, *Forget it.* They're providing a service that the person is paying for – both sides need to be in agreement. I think that at some point what was an exchange lost the essence of exchange – you give me that and I'll give you this in return: money, beans, cheese, protection, whatever. Money makes the world go 'round. Money also distances us from the product and the labor it takes to create it and the work it takes to ship it and the work it takes to run a business. Money talks. But money only talks if people choose to listen. Money can't buy everything.

We encounter this situation in our schools, as well. The education system and more directly, teachers, provide a service to our students, who are in recent trends referred to as "customers." There is an expectation that teachers cater to different students' needs, learning styles, skill levels, etc. Having taught eighth grade Language Arts (reading and writing) for four years, I definitely see the importance of finding different ways to explain ideas and making modifications to reach each student. But I think there is a fundamental error in this logic: the student is passively receiving and the teacher is actively giving, rather than it being a give-and-take. What about the student being an active participant in his learning? What about seeking out knowledge because you thirst for it and respecting those who are willing to impart what they know to you? What happened to studying not because you have a test in the morning or because your parents force you to, but because you want to learn?

So no, as of now, I don't plan to hand out fish. I will stubbornly stick to the mission of teaching people to fish or, better yet, helping them teach themselves to fish. Those are the dancers I want to share an embrace with – the ones who feel the dance and are aware of my needs and desires as their partner in a collaborative undertaking, the ones who dare to venture outside the lines with me, the ones who make me feel heard and understood and have something interesting to say in our conversation, the ones who aren't worried about getting lost, because they know that together we can find each other again and together is the only way we can dance a tango.

I am because I choose

From where to live to what to eat for dinner, to whether you should stay an extra day just because you're having such a good time, even if you already have a bus ticket to leave. You can't do it all – *todo no se puede.* So you have to choose.

Rodolfo Dinzel says that a teacher, like a doctor, needs to keep in mind that you can't give the student a whole bottle of medicine – take this. You have to know how to prescribe just the right dose.

He also says that as a student he realized that he always left with half of what the teacher said – make sure you leave with the half that works for you. *"No hay que confiar completamente en ninguna persona,"* Rodolfo told me one day, "You should never completely trust any one person." Always have a back door, a secret escape route, he said. It's true. If we find someone who seems to be an authority on a subject, a genius, an idol, a *maestro*, it's easy to begin to take everything they say as ultimate truth. But having the option of saying "no," makes your yes's worth something. When we stop choosing, when we forget that truth is relative and right is relative and we stop thinking for ourselves, we no longer learn, we're no longer part of the process, we're no longer present.

As my dad, Arcady Condrea, used to say, you and only you are responsible for the decisions you make and you will be the one who has to deal with the consequences. Ask for advice, then choose for yourself and choose wisely. Intelligence is knowing how to choose.

A mi maestro, Rodolfo Dinzel –

que me abrió las puertas,
que me mostró otra manera de ser,
que creó un lugar mágico,
una casa lejos de mi casa,
donde tantos buscan refugio
de este mundo tan rígido,
que me ayudó a buscar mi propio camino,
que me enseñó a pensar por mí misma,
a ver lo que es y no lo que yo pienso que debería ser.
– ¡Gracias!

To my maestro (my teacher), Rodolfo Dinzel –

who opened doors for me,
who showed me another way to be,
who created a magical space,
a home far from home,
where so many seek refuge
from our rigid world,
who encouraged me to seek my own path,
who taught me to think for myself,
to see what is rather than what I think should be.
– Thank you!

A Lifelong Student

Being a teacher is not the end of learning; it's the beginning of another stage. It means that I approach learning with the intention of sharing. "There is no such thing as teaching," says Lydia Condrea, "there is only learning." It's a give and take, always.

Taking on the challenge of teaching, of sharing your knowledge and your experience is a lot of responsibility. One thing you say could change someone's life. Yet you can't live walking on eggshells or being so careful that you end up saying nothing at all. Although I suggest staying away from absolute statements that include words like "never" and "always," all you can do is impart what you know and have found useful for you.[93] The best that you can give is your very best, and since the idea is to keep growing as an individual, your very best changes over time.

If we, as students, remember to think critically, we can liberate our teachers from the mold of some superhuman all-knowing being. Watch out for those who know "everything," especially those who want to make sure you know that they know "everything." To paraphrase Socrates, he who knows everything, knows very little. He who knows that he doesn't know everything knows at least that the quest continues.

"You are your own best teacher," writes John Lee on his web site, AllSeattleTango.com. It's about taking responsibility for your learning and being an active participant in the process – figuring out how to ask the right questions and discerning what's useful for you.

---

[93] Absolute statements seem to imply that you are the authority, but tango is a popular dance – leave yourself room to grow.

I spent a lot of time being a "good" student, but recently, I realized that seeking my teacher's nod of approval is not enough for me. I don't just want to be a good student; I want to learn. So I changed my approach – I started asking questions and humbling myself enough to say, I don't know or What would you suggest? or How do you explain this? And some were questions that I obviously knew the answer to, that I knew *my* answer to, but the point of taking someone else's class is to find out how she explains it.

In the debating spirit of my Grandpa Constantin "Carl" Condrea, who found it hard to resist a heated argument, a good discussion is worth more than a standing ovation. I have been fortunate enough throughout my journey, to encounter viewpoints that contradict mine. Fortunate because they have challenged me to choose, to reevaluate and shape and ultimately strengthen my own vision.

Knowledge is finite, whereas intelligence is infinite. Seek intelligence over knowledge. Reserve the right to make mistakes and learn from them. I am a student and a teacher and the day that I stop being a student, *el día que ya no busco más* – the day that I stop searching, will be the last day I teach.

Build your own castle

> *Más vale rancho propio que palacio ajeno* – a shack of your own is better than somebody else's palace

Since I managed to hold a marker in my hand, I've loved to draw and paint. I'd paint and paint and paint. A series of houses, then people, then Venetian canals. And my Mom told me something very important: too much can ruin a painting – part of creating art is knowing when to stop. Rather than telling me when she thought I should stop, she encouraged me to determine that moment for myself.

Life is like that, too. People can give you all kinds of advice, but they can't paint your path for you – you have to seek it out yourself. And it's not always easy forging your own path. It involves a lot of searching and trying and grasping at the unknown, a lot of self-reflection and learning to have faith in yourself.

Each tango is unique, like each step, like each breath, like each moment in your life. You can't be someone else. You can't repeat or recreate or replicate. Trust your intuition; test things out. See what feels good to you. Collect all the golden nuggets people give you – in each class, in each conversation, in each embrace – and build your own castle. By choosing what you like and what fits you, little by little, you build your own dance.

Glossary

abrazo – an embrace, a hug

boleo – a move where your free leg swivels around you or swings straight out and returns, either along the floor or in the air

cabeceo – a way of making eye contact to invite someone to and to accept an invitation to dance

embellishments/adornments – stylistic touches one can add to the dance

entregarse – to give oneself

gancho – a movement that involves "hooking" your leg around your partner

giro – turn

medialunas – "half moons," small croissant-like pastries traditionally eaten for breakfast or throughout the day in much of Argentina

milonga – a social gathering where people dance tango and other dances; a genre of music; a dance (similar to tango)

mirada – gaze, eye contact before you dance (the *cabeceo*)

ocho – spiral movements that look like a figure 8; eight

sacada – a move that gives the illusion of kicking your partner's leg or foot out of the way

tanda – a set of 3-5 (usually 4) songs, which you generally dance with one partner

tango – the music, the dance

tanguera/o – a person who dances tango

"thank you" – saying "thank you" on the dance floor in tango generally means that you are done dancing with that person for the time being or for the rest of the evening

Notes to the Reader:

Dear Reader,

This book wrote itself. It is the product of many disconnected yet so very connected moments of inspiration, moments in which I was driven to write by the sheer impulse of having something to say, something that had to come out and dance with the white background of my computer screen – words jumbled on napkins, interrupted conversations to jot down ideas, startled friends in the face of my nearly jumping at the excitement of encountering yet another concept to play with. A cascade of ideas, a waterfall of words, a conversation with my mentors, my friends, with myself. You hold in your hands my contribution to the larger exchange about tango and human relationships.

Welcome to the conversation.

More Notes:

My use of **gender-specific pronouns,** "he" for leads and "she" for follows, respectively, is for the purpose of convenience and clarity, not meant to negate the fact that both men and women can lead and follow and sometimes it doesn't even matter who's doing what because it flows. In general, they can be used interchangeably. Please substitute what makes sense for you.

When I put text in **Spanish** first, it's because I originally wrote it in Spanish or because I like it in Spanish. In some cases, I offer an artistic rather than a direct translation, to better express the ideas that might otherwise be lost in translation.

Thank You

To each person who has shared an embrace with me.

A Rodolfo Dinzel (mi maestro), Anita Postorino, Rosita y toda mi gente, mis compañeros del Estudio Dinzel por cultivar mi creatividad y ser mi familia lejos de mi casa.

To all the teachers – named in this book and not – who have shaped me and my dance.

To my students, for inspiring me to contemplate your questions and giving me reason to continue this quest.

To my writing students at Frederick Douglass K-8 in Philadelphia and at Asa Mercer Middle School and The Northwest School in Seattle for inspiring me to write and grow with you.

To my sponsor, Neil Zussman, without whose support this book could not have been published.

To Lull Mengesha, for your guidance throughout the self-publishing process.

To my editors – Lydia Condrea, Terry Benioff, and Inna Condrea – who gave me invaluable feedback. I could not have done this without you!

To Carlos D. Alvarez for checking my Spanish, and to my Facebook editors for all the translation and grammar help.

To Thomas and Ann and everyone at Chocolati Café on Greenwood, for letting me sit for hours and feeding me chocolate, lattés and bacon, cheese, and green onion bagels.

To the Seattle tango community for receiving me with open arms whenever I touch base here.

To my friends, in the U.S., in Argentina, and everywhere in between, for your support, hugs, and stimulating conversations. It takes a village – thank you for being my village. A Débora Chiodi por adoptarme y compartir tu familia y tus amigos conmigo. To my dear, dear friends in Seattle for being there for me all these years. A special shout out to Faye, Erin, and Pete.

To my family, near and far, for standing by me and believing in me. Mulţumesc, Mama şi Tata, Inna-Cipo T-M, my "twin" brother Daniel, Bunica Raia, Bunica Caty, Bunicul Carl, şi Tanti Genya.

And to all the many people I have not mentioned here – each person I asked for feedback on a detail here a detail there, how would you translate this, each conversation, each interaction that inspired the creation of this book. Thank you! Thank you so very, very much!

Made in the USA
Middletown, DE
23 June 2020